laugh

at

love

AN UNREMEMOIR BY: EVERY GIRL

DEDICATION

To all the fools in these stories who gave me the material for this book and led me to learn such valuable lessons in life.

More importantly, to all of the amazing people in my life who put up with me through all of it.

ACKNOWLEDGMENTS

Music moves my soul and no copyright infringement was intended. Acknowledgements throughout the book are to the best of my ability and knowledge.

"Her tongue is like the Devil, when she tries to concentrate.
She says she don't want marriage, but she still believes in fate.
And she stands her ground defiantly, but cries when she's alone.
Oh, she's every girl I've ever known."

Turnpike Troubadours, Every Girl

Chapter 1

If only I could tattoo every terrible or all-wrong-for-me guy I've ever encountered. Nothing dramatic, terribly painful or ill-willed; maybe just a small black "X," a tiny scarlet "A," a barely visible "No," or even a little stab wound on their shoulder (...a message to both them and me). Just a quick, visual indicator that I should run like hell, not that I really need help in the running department— just ask my mother. It just seems it could be a helpful time saver for aging "girls" like me who are so over the bullshit of dating.

I use the word "girl," not just because I haven't yet mastered the art of adulthood, but also because the word "woman" makes me feel ancient. Most people are quick to admonish me for stating I'm old. Yet, somehow, I'm suddenly no longer the vivacious, youthful "girl" who loosely clung to her infinitely single life, while others both pitied me and tried to instill hope at the same time:

That's ok, honey, you don't need a man.

Good for you! They're only trouble.

Atta girl, not settling!

You're so young; you've got so much time.

If we're being honest, and it seems as though I am: none of these really ever seemed all that comforting (and not just because they were delivered with excessive amounts of pity), but I had to roll with it in any and every social or family setting (still do). Simply because *I know; I'm not worried!* Sounds so much better and allows people to feel a little more comfortable than *Well, God, I hope so because I get older every day, still never having been in a serious relationship. I must clearly have unresolved issues I can't work out, and it's making me doubt everything about myself because no one can pinpoint exactly what's wrong with me.*

Now don't get me wrong, most of the time these days I know exactly who I am and what I want, and I stand firm in that. I'm actually pretty damn proud of who I've turned out to be, and you can rest assured this is no self-help book. It's more like a memoir, or hopefully an unrememoir of men in the dating world these days and the reasons I still find myself alone.

At this point in my life, all my friends are married, engaged, pregnant, or parents. [Insert dramatic pitiful sigh here.] This is the part of the FRIENDS episode where I'm Joey, and everyone else has moved on with their lives and settled down with *the one*. This is the part where I'm supposed to kick and scream because *I'm going to die alone!!*

Well, here's the good news— In the long, triumphant journey of finding myself, I came to realize I'm pretty great, and I don't need someone else to fill a void or make me feel whole. That being said, I do want to find someone. Who doesn't want to be loved and adored? (Yes, Mom, even I do.) Some days it's tough, some days it's lonely, and some days it's absolutely miserable waiting on that someone; someone who sees in you the things that you yourself, your friends, and your family are all able to see. For whatever reason though, the endless line of idiots, jerks, or almost possibilities just can't stick around long enough to notice.

Some of the almost possibilities may have caught glimpse, but something just wasn't right or the chemistry wasn't there. And after all of this soul-searching and man-cruising, why would I settle for any less than I, this awesome person, deserves?

To some, this makes me picky. To others, I must be damaged. To distant family, I'm immediately deemed a lesbian. To my mother, I'm difficult and stubborn, refusing to grant her the grandchildren she's entitled to (that she can just as easily obtain from any of my three brothers, so back off). To my brothers, this made me easy to look out for when I was younger and didn't have a father to scare boys off. Somewhere, surely, my dad looked down on me and laughed, watching me scare them off myself—although to clarify, I never intentionally scared them off, and usually it meant more tears than laughter for me. It wasn't always easy and mostly just felt to me like a long, lonely road. Luckily now, I'm able to see that the road had me heading in the direction I need to go.

In hindsight, I believe I was truly wise beyond my years. I actually think I knew that all along. My mom is certain she did something terribly wrong to make me so cynical, but the truth is, she made me brave, sensible, and slightly guarded—all the tools I needed to survive and grow into the woman I needed to become, without completely slutting it up, breaking inside, or ruining my life.

With these skills, I have been able to endure over a decade of terrible dating (or non-dating) experiences, and I'm ready and willing to share the tell-tale signs of a guy you'll be wasting your time with. Tattoos, if you will, of warning signals to you that you should just keep moving.

Now if you're anything like me, you'll finish this book wondering, *"Well where the hell am I supposed to meet anyone then?"* or *"Are there any good guys out there?"*

Well, like I said, this is no self-help book, and I still don't have those answers, but I'll be damned if I end up with one of these guys, continuing to feel like shit about myself or questioning how I can be better for them. No, if I'm going to feel like shit, it will be self-doubt on my own terms. I refuse to let myself not feel good enough for someone anymore. I highly recommend that. It was the biggest step along my journey, with the greatest results.

As we proceed into the parade of fools, please keep in mind that I'm not a man-hater. I love guys. I grew up surrounded by brothers, and their friends, and my guy friends, and step-brothers, and cousins, and family friends, all of which were guys. I have always been kind of a guys' girl, which I used to think would work in my favor when it came to dating, as I'm very easy going, love sports, dogs, and outdoor activities. However, instead, that quickly backfired into numerous friend-zone situations when it came to crushes I had through the years. Through that process, I ended up with countless extremely close guy friends, who I had to then coach through crazy bitch after crazy bitch after crazy bitch.

It was exhausting, but the guys in my life, especially my brothers, have set the bar extremely high for my expectations of men. Therefore, I know that what I'm looking for exists. I'm not being unreasonable. I'm asking for very little: respect, attraction, and humor. Why is it so hard to find?

I'm sometimes inclined to blame women for being willing to be the mindless chess pieces these guys are obviously expecting, but then these guys shouldn't think it's an option anyway, nor should anyone want that kind of one-sided relationship. I can only hope that women who become what a man wants them to be are just going through an insecure phase or tough time and that they will grow out of it. Nothing makes me sadder for a woman than watching them disappear into someone else's life and their identity fading away. However, more than sad, it makes me angry. A guy should never create that environment for someone, but the girl really needs to stand up for herself and do what makes her happy or get out. Whatever the reason, there are now an abundance of guys who expect girls to just sit on the back burner and be whatever the guy wants them to be. I have no interest in being in a relationship like this, and I would hope most people don't want to.

Perhaps we can all avoid ending up in situations like the ones I have managed to find myself in and avoid the assholes who expect to mold you into whatever passive, silent partner they are expecting to control. Obviously, I can't speak for everyone, but I can describe the terrible dating situations I've encountered and encourage you to think twice and heed warning when you notice the signs that precede the ridiculousness that lies ahead. Sometimes when life throws you curveballs and it feels like your dating life is a joke, all you can do is sit back and laugh. Just remember that it's all part of the journey, and you just have to embrace it as it comes and enjoy the ride. That's what I'm doing now: laughing at love and the absurd dating experiences life has thrown my way.

Chapter 2

The "Unicorn"

"I know that I can't take no more, it ain't no lie. I want to see you out that door, baby, bye bye bye."
'NSYNC, *Bye Bye Bye*

Let's get right to it. Sign number one that things won't work out... not remembering his name, or he yours. I have a firm rule that I don't give my number to anyone unless they know my name. Too often in the drunken scene of hormones and Vegas bombs, a guy will ask some girl for their number, as is orchestrated protocol in "the bar scene."

Raise your hand if you don't have someone saved as "Joe Pub Fiction" or "Jared? Tall Guy" saved in your phone. If your hand isn't raised, either you're lying or-- Way to go! For real, serious props. I wish I could say the same. I have ended up with more than a few guys who were unmemorable enough to require an accompanying adjective or location to help me keep them straight.

Along those same lines, my friends and I have developed another term, used only in the highest of esteem: *unicorn*. This phrase was born out of the idea that unicorns don't exist, neither do perfect guys (or girls). So a *unicorn* is someone you either haven't met or have met briefly enough to not really know anything about them. It's in those moments you are able to build up and create this entire life for them in which they are the perfect counterpart for you. Whether you see them from afar or in pictures, hear about them from a friend, or meet them in a quick encounter, they can momentarily be the perfection you've been waiting for. You can dream up an entire life with this fictional character that they may or may not be (they aren't).

While I don't discourage the use of *unicorn,* I just warn that you should proceed with caution. It's a slippery slope where you may fall too hard into the false image of them, that if you do in time meet them and spend time with them—that image will begin to cloud your judgment of who they really are. You'll find yourself granting extra chances and overlooking things that should never be acceptable. However, it is mostly fun and rarely stems into something real, so the elusive *unicorn* is both a fun pastime, as well as a beacon of hope.

The problems only arise when you attempt to see that unicorn in the light of day. It's never as pretty. In my case, it was more like a mutilated centaur by the time it was all said and done.

The unicorn in this particular case was "the lawyer." (Not important enough to recall his name… no really I couldn't remember. I had to look it up in my phone.) He will forevermore be referred to as "the lawyer." Honestly, he may be the worst of all so I decided to jump right in with his atrocious story.

***

This story begins at rodeo cook-off... Oh, you are unfamiliar with this setting? Allow me to paint a quick picture: row after row of endless giant party tents, each containing its own parking lot party with hundreds of people, bottomless drinks, and loud music. Acres of these parties are surrounded by carnival rides, concerts, and party people clad in jeans and boots for a four day long carefree country-style bash. It's the perfect place for someone like me (a city girl with country roots) to meet a guy. I'm in my element and can really be myself, plus everyone for the most part has similar interests. This particular year happened to be my favorite experience there, and on the third night of four that I was in attendance, I arrived midafternoon with two of my girlfriends, easing into the evening after a long couple of days.

So, there we were, 24-years-old: a blonde, a brunette, and a red head, ready to see where the night took us. We started with a few drinks on the way, then a few drinks in our party's tent, then off to check out a new party. A friend of a friend got us into an "exclusive" party tent. Anyone who has been to anything like that knows that "exclusive" just means long ass lines and no room to move. Lines to get in, lines for the bathroom, lines for drinks—it's actually the kind of thing I hate, but you do what you do for free booze and hot guys. Am I right? Luckily, these exclusive inconveniences are a little easier to manage for three cute girls. Ten minutes into a thirty-minute line to the entrance, some guys recognized us and pulled us up to the front of the line. Layne and Amber had to pee immediately. They headed straight for the fifteen-minute bathroom line, while I offered to grab us drinks.

As I wandered up towards the bar, I couldn't help but sigh heavily as I realized there was yet another line for the bar. I must have sighed heavily enough to catch the eye of the two guys currently ordering at the bar (of course not intentionally). They invited me up to the bar with them and allowed me to order drinks for my crew, even ordered a few extra for us so we wouldn't have to hop right back in line. As everything settled out and the girls returned to claim their drinks, we managed to find a nearby free table to hover around as we began the introductions. As we did so, I realize I've happened into a 6' 6" extremely handsome stallion with a sexy Southern drawl and perfectly snug jeans over his size 16 boots. Although I may not really have a "type," if I did— he'd be it. I mean damn!

It appeared that I too, was his type, as we immediately jumped into witty banter, movie quotes, and music trivia. It was perfection. In a matter of minutes, it seemed we knew each other well, and we were dancing the night away. Shortly after we inched our way around a crowded dance floor, we were back with our crew leaning in closely to talk and drunkenly gazing into each other's eyes. Our instant connection was so obvious to the others that Layne and Amber wasted no time snapping pictures of us laughing, him placing his cowboy hat on my head, and us unable to take our eyes off of each other. From there it all started to become slightly blurry, but his friend managed to put his number in my phone and saved it as "Hot Tall Guy"— See, guys do it too—and me and the girls were ready to head on to the next tent. He and I had briefly discussed meeting up the next night, which was the point of exchanging numbers. We sent a text or two between that night and following day, but that was the extent of our time together at cook off.

Ladies night didn't end there though, and the fun

continued for a few more hours. Eventually, we decided to head home and stood in the longest line ever for the bus. For some reason, people kept thinking they could cut in front of us to get closer to the front. The girls and I had enough of that crap and against all better judgement, we went on to nearly fight a drunk man. He just happened to be about the 10th person who attempted to cut to the front of the line. It turns out ten was one too many. We blocked the line lengthwise and sassed him about proceeding, destroyed his excuse for the bathroom as we pointed it out in the other direction. Just to get the point across, Amber flicked his ear. Did I mention we were drunk? This was one of the dumbest things we could've done to a drunk strange man in Houston, but we were too far gone. We came out alive, thank God, as his girlfriend arrived to yell at him, and he suddenly had bigger issues than us. More importantly, we were successful, and he didn't get to cut; ultimately, the strangers around us who had admonished us for our attempts and looked at us like we were crazy ended up applauding our heroic behavior, *traitors*.

The rest of the weekend was spent catching up with old friends and never again seeing that perfect statuesque creature I ultimately deemed my "Unicorn." He would live in my mind as perfection, despite his terrible texting grammar, which I was willing to overlook for all of his other flawless qualities.

About a week later, I received what was clearly a drunk text of song lyrics, rap lyrics to be exact from my Unicorn: "I'm too fly, you know this. Lemme give yo ass a checklist." I found it hilarious and wanted to play along, even though his unicorn status was quickly disappearing more each time he said words. I googled the lyrics, picked a different song from the same artist, and rattled off some similar lyrics in order to keep the banter going. His response was simply "perfect." That was the last I heard from him.

***

     Cut to me: maybe a month or so later, going out for a night on the town with my roommate Jessi. For some reason, she and I tend to have the best luck with free drinks and male attention when we go out together. It's pretty entertaining, as we couldn't be more opposite: she a tiny, five-foot-nothing, blonde with curly hair and a serial monogamist, me a 5' 10" brunette with straight hair and perpetually single. We rarely pay for drinks, often end up dancing, and almost never give out our numbers (and if Jessi does, it's fake). Nevertheless, we always have a blast, and we rarely got to do it anymore. We finally made time for it, and as usual, it was a roaring success. The whole night, I had my eye on this tall guy across the bar, and he seemed to notice. It took a while, but we finally managed to "bump into" each other and strike up conversation.

     A little while later, Jessi and I decided to call it a night. He got my number as we headed out the door. We had more than enough to drink and took a cab home as planned. While on the way back, I get a text from Unicorn. It took a few minutes and a text or two to realize that Unicorn and this guy from the bar that night were the same person.

     Sign number one to run like hell: if neither of you remember each other and exchange numbers twice. It's not fate—it's fucked up. *Run.*

The young and desperate version of me chose to see it as fate, and would go on to tell this story as if it were the beginning of some twisted and silly, yet sweetly awesome star-crossed love story. *Dumbass.*

I went on to discover that he was a lawyer and from a small town near our family's country house in the middle of nowhere. He also had a gorgeous apartment right in between my apartment and midtown with a beautiful view of the city from his balcony, where we would go on to spend a few nights drinking, chatting, and more gazing into each other's eyes. It was all so perfect, he was regaining Unicorn status. We went on a couple of dates and met up after drunken nights out. It started out so well, but the first night I stayed at his place I told him I had to be somewhere early so I needed a ride home. The bastard would not get up and drive me. I was only about a mile and a half from home and it was around 6:00 in the morning, so I decided to just walk rather than be a difficult bitch or call a cab. I was in wedges (because I could be with this giant human) and my feet hurt like hell by the time I got back. I was pretty pissed that he wouldn't get up for five minutes to take me home. This was pre-Uber, so it was a real jackass move. The next time (there shouldn't have been a next time), he got to sleep a little later and was willing to drive me home. So kind.

We went to a movie together, and unfortunately I quickly realized that hanging out with him sober was nearly painful. Thank God the movie kept us from having to talk for most of our time together. He was so judgmental and such a dick about every little meaningless thing. After the movie, I tried to have an intellectual discussion about how the movie (*Gatsby*) spoke about the human condition and the selfishness of our society as a whole. He acted like I was an idiot and that I made no sense.

After that, I was pretty much over it because like I said I have no patience for being made to feel like less than I am or less than someone else. However, a couple of nights later I was out with friends and so was he. I met him back at his place after the bars closed. It was apparently his birthday. I wasn't willing to have sex with him at this point, especially since I realized more and more how much he sucked as a person. He was frustrated that I still wouldn't (after hanging out four times across two whole weeks). He argued that it was his birthday, which just made me less interested. He got pissed and told me that I couldn't stay the night then, and held the front door open. I, being the sassy bitch that I am, yelled "Fine!" and stormed out, thinking he would call me back in, but instead heard the door slam. As I got further down the hall towards the elevator, I thought surely he'd come after me and stop me, since it was 3:30 in the morning. Nothing. Still nothing as I walked out of the apartment complex. I stomped down the sidewalk towards my apartment, a walk I already knew thanks to his initial asshole move.

I got about 50 yards away from the complex and was fuming with rage at this point. I couldn't help but text him: "Really?!" His response being: "Don't try to make me look like an asshole, you did this."

... Seriously. Can't make this shit up.

Obviously we never spoke again. Lesson learned there: Unicorns don't exist, and once an asshole, always an asshole. Take notes, *laugh*, move on...

Chapter 3

The Thursday Night Guy

"Do you remember when I met you, what I whispered in your ear? Be my temporary angel and I'll be your love for just one day. Hold me for a moment, let the moment fade away."
Pat Green, *Temporary Angel*

Through the years, I've encountered a few different variations of this guy. The first being the obvious and truly literal Thursday Night Guy, the others were sequels of the same type of guy.

I had recently changed careers and had a Friday off with no work and no training. I was getting to the point in my life where going out was exhausting and took days to recover from, so I rarely went out—especially on weeknights. However, when this particular responsibility-free Thursday night rolled around, I was really feeling up to a fun night out.

Throughout this book, it may seem like I party a lot and end up with plenty of guys, but just to remind you: this was over about a decade, so there were plenty of draughts in between. In fact for this particular story, it had been almost a year since I'd even kissed a guy. A year. *So back off.*

Point being, I decided to go out on Thursday night, mostly to celebrate my new career and my instantly more joyous life (leaving a painfully miserable job). I had talked a couple of friends into going: my childhood friend and previous roommate Chad and our relatively new friend Brandon, both gay, and both troopers to stay out with me and play wingman for hours. We had dinner and a few drinks before going out in Midtown. We weren't there long, and they were about ready to call it a night, as Chad was tired and did have to work the next day, and Brandon had just finished taking the bar that day (therefore had been celebrating/drinking all day already). Just before they were ready to go, a nearby group of guys popped up on our radar, and before I knew it, I was talking to a good-looking tall (*yes, you're sensing a tall theme*) guy in a Canada t-shirt, and I pled with despairing eyes to my wingmen to stick around just a little longer.

As they trudged to the bar, Canada and I hit it off right away chatting about jobs we had hated and left, how he was from NY and his sister bought him said Canada shirt, as well as our shared love of volleyball. He invited me to play in a tournament with their co-ed team in a couple of weeks, so we exchanged numbers. He recalled my name, so I willingly added my number to his phone and allowed him to save it however he chose. He struggled for a minute before sending me his contact info, claiming he was "bad at phones…" whatever that means. *Sign number one. It was 2014, what twenty- something in 2014 can't work their own cell phone?* Meanwhile, his friends had disappeared, so he left to meet back up with them. I hustled over to my boys at the bar to thank them for the patience and grant them approval that we could leave. However, I underestimated what one more drink would do, and now they were ready to rage a little longer.

We all ordered another drink and started dancing around, when all of a sudden the dark clouds (this is no metaphor, literal dark clouds) that had lingered all night burst out in an outrageous downpour. Bright lightning, followed by immediate booming thunder lit up the torrential cascade. The bar went crazy, the power went out momentarily, and it was suddenly an epic Thursday night. We were essentially trapped in the bar. I began receiving playful texts from Canada about the crazy weather and how tragic it was that the elements were keeping us apart. He heroically offered to brave the storm and run across the street to come back to me so we can be "trapped" together. Obviously, I was unopposed. A year, people. Chad helped me with playful banter replies, and in the final text where he asks if he should go for it, I offered to have a towel waiting if he made it through the storm.

Here I go… was his reply. Shit. Why would I promise a towel? Damn it, Chad. I hustled into to the bathroom and pulled a single paper towel. Nailed it.

He ran in, beyond soaked, removing each shoe and pouring a pool of water onto the floor. I dabbed him with the useless paper towel and smiled shamelessly, as we ordered another drink.

Normally I'm not a big fan of bar make-outs. Well, I should clarify. I enjoy laughing at them, but I don't normally enjoy being involved in them. However, with too much alcohol, a hot enough guy, and a long enough dry spell, sometimes you just can't argue with it (especially if he swoops in from the rain in true chick-flick-fashion). There's only so much willpower one can maintain.

It turned out to be one hell of a Thursday night. The

rain lightened up just enough that Chad and Brandon decided to sprint back to their car. I granted them permission, as I nodded I was fine to stay with my new friend. Evidently, Chad made it back to the nearly-flooded car with Brandon nowhere to be found. He laughed thinking to himself that the rain must've taken him. Sadly it had, as he went back for him and found that he had tripped and fallen and couldn't quite regroup to make it back to the car. So hilarious and sad. Sorry, Brandon.

Meanwhile, back at the bar, Canada looked me up and down. I raised an eyebrow, as if to question his actions. He said "I'm just seeing what kind of shoes you're wearing to see if you'll make it if we have to run in the rain. I live right across the street."

I laughed and nodded, but fairly warned him, "That's fine, but I'll let you know now that I'm not going to have sex with you. I thought I'd be honest and give you an out. I can still take a cab home." I've learned that the sooner I divulge this to someone, the better off we both end up. I just am not crazy about the idea of random sex. It's just not my thing.

He smiled, grabbed my hand, and said, "Totally fine, let's go." We each took one last swig of our beers and left them half full on the bar. He pulled me by the hand and guided me across the street to a complex where my friend used to live. Lucky that I was familiar with it, because with the rain I would've never seen where I was going. As we neared his apartment, he mentioned, "Oh I should warn you too; there's someone sleeping on my couch. A friend of mine is in town for work and he needed a place to stay."

As we stumbled through the door, I took a quick glance at the numbers, and prayed that my blurred vision still allowed me to read it correctly. I typed a quick text to two of my best girl friends with the complex name and apartment number followed by "In case I die..." *I'm so responsible.*

My untrusting nature is what always kept me from becoming a big fan of one night stands. I never feel that comfortable, I don't really trust anyone's intentions, and I'm always too worried that they think they are winning or that I'm just one of the dumb girls I pity who will do whatever a guy wants, even if it's something I want. On this particular Thursday, all the makings were right and it was just what I wanted. I deemed that it was being done on my terms and I had already set the limits, so I just went with it—without regret. I knew it was going nowhere, and I was ok with it.

He really did have a friend sleeping on his couch, and he had work the next morning. However, we had a really good night. We actually talked quite a bit and had a lot of fun together. If it weren't going to be a one night thing, I could see being interested. To be fair, I was pretty drunk and he may have sucked, but it was the attention I wanted for the night, and I was pretty proud of it. His friend left early that morning to catch a flight home. Despite having to work, Canada still had the decency to drive me home and kiss me goodbye.

I was perfectly content with that being the extent of it, and we proceeded to only text if we were out in Midtown and a few drinks in. He, like clockwork, only texted on Thursdays, when I was never actually out. I went out one more Thursday around that time and played my role of "Thursday Night Girl" by sending him a casual text. Sadly he wasn't out that night and waited two days to text back to let me know that he couldn't respond because he had been sick... *Sign number two: anyone who takes longer than a few hours to reply is super sketchy.*

Thank God I didn't give a shit or he would've screwed me up even more by doing what Thursday Night Guys do: giving just enough hope to keep you on the line, and then making you feel dumb for hanging on. I knew better by now than to fall for his games. Short, well-timed responses are all he got from me, too, just to keep him interested enough to know that he didn't use me or "win" the game. I love games, but HATE the ones that are of the dating nature. They are an exhausting waste of time, brain power, and emotion. So I put very little thought into the connection, and just accepted it as flattery that I still heard from him most Thursday nights for a while. I was even more tickled when each week, the texts got earlier in the night. I continued to receive a dozen or so texts in the weeks that followed that night, but it just was not in the cards (especially because who can go out on Thursdays that frequently?).

Obviously it's a problem if you only hear from someone when they're drinking, and this is the essence of the "Thursday Night Guy." They are selfish to the point where they think you only exist when they're ready for you. This is a lesson I learned well with another variation of the Thursday Night Guy.

***

The original "Thursday Night Guy" was the third guy I

dated with the same name (yes-this becomes a red flag in itself), and this particular one will henceforth be referred to as TNG.

I actually met this one a few years earlier through my roommate, Jessi, and her boyfriend. He and TNG were old high school friends, and he had just recently moved to Houston, around the same time Jessi and I moved back to town and started living together. We went out one night to a concert at a local country bar with a big group of their friends. TNG and I hit it off right away, singing along and dancing to some of my favorite songs.

We started texting and hanging out almost immediately, and I started to see potential for a real relationship, which rarely happens. We had plenty in common, most importantly a passion for music (which is my life) and we just kind of clicked. Just as things seemed to be progressing, he pulled away, and I started only hearing from him around Thursday of every week. I was in no rush to be in a relationship, so I went along with it. However, I found myself further annoyed each week as he had less and less to say to me during the week and expected me to just show up every Thursday and stay the night.

It got the point where I was no longer willing to show up at his beck and call when he was ready to spend a few hours with me, so I decided to put an end to my feeling used. I asked him about his lack of interest the rest of the week, and he flipped out. He proceeded to respond to my one sentence question with a novel dictating that I was crazy, and he doesn't know why I'm pushing for a relationship. I couldn't help but laugh at his preposterous presumptions and never responded. I'm far better than having to listen to someone calling me crazy and needy, two things I pride myself on never having been.

Growing up around only boys taught me real quick that crazy, needy girls were pathetic and something I'd never be. I can say there are times I've felt crazy thoughts coming on, and I run from any situation that makes me feel that way because I refuse to let those thoughts materialize. So for someone so selfish and neurotic to imply that I was the crazy one was absolute bullshit and beyond requiring a response.

I didn't talk to him again for about a month, and then I ran into him at a big music festival with Jessi. I was in a good place by then, and when he wanted to discuss rekindling our flame, I kindly told him we could make out that night if we could never talk about it again. He didn't like my sassy reply and wanted a real conversation. He eventually got one at the end of the night, where he didn't get to hear what he'd hoped. I went on to let him know he wouldn't get a second chance, because crazy was the wrong route to take with me.

The happy ending here (for me) is that the next girl he dated (and is still currently dating) is truly a crazy bitch. Obviously crazy was what he wanted all along, and I guess that's what he was trying to spark in me with his dramatic reply. He's now with a girl who hates living here, but moved here for him from Arizona within weeks of meeting him in a bar, threatens him with ultimatums about proposing, and faked a robbery at her apartment to act like it was unsafe for her to live alone so that she could force herself into living with him. He wanted crazy, he got it—and it sure as hell was never going to be me.

Point being, like I previously mentioned, games suck, but if you have to play, make sure you're playing on your terms. Don't allow yourself to get played, by allowing someone else to dictate when and where you "get" to spend time with them. Thursday Night Guys, whether dating you or a casual hook up, will find a way to haunt you and belittle you until you decide to call your own shots. Also, do us all a favor and never play into the crazy a guy tries to hurl your way. This world definitely doesn't need any more crazy bitches, and you shouldn't aspire to be one.

Chapter 4

The All But Your Boyfriend

"Better gimme that title, title…"
Meghan Trainor, *Title*

This next guy is full of red flags that I was too blind to see at the time. He was Same Name #2 (the second guy of three I dated with the same name). I stayed with him far longer than I should have, but I really thought I'd found someone I'd actually call my boyfriend. Unfortunately, he was ultimately *all but my boyfriend*.

I met him while working a game day job for an NFL team. I always had big plans of working for a sports team doing something along the lines of community relations or event coordinating, if not sports journalism. This game day job was one of the many steps I took in that journey that eventually led me nowhere but disappointment, but that's not the point. While working that job, I had a blast and met some really great people along the way, some of which are still my friends today.

One of the guys I worked with was (yep, you guessed it) tall, cute, sweet, and funny. What more could I ask for? Towards the end of our first season working together, we all went out together one night and ended up having a lot of fun.

Nicole, my best friend from that job, was with us, and we were joined by the cop that I worked closely with all season who had a huge crush on Nicole, as well as the guy who was my future non-boyfriend, and a few others. We went out on a Sunday after the game, and it turns out there's not a ton to do, but we found a bar where we could two step and play pool. We were all set.

We shut the bar down and ended up across the street, back at Nicole's for a few more hours of fun. Nicole's "cop boyfriend" sweetly wrote her a cute "check yes or no" note so they were happily enjoying each other's company. *Gag.* Meanwhile, my guy and I had danced all night (he was just ok at dancing, after swearing for weeks he was the best— *sign number one perhaps*) and we ended up snuggled up at Nicole's for the night.

In the weeks to follow, we would develop something pretty great, despite being half-way long distance. I was still in college about an hour and a half away, but I was back every weekend for the games anyway. I hadn't/ still haven't really had a serious relationship. Obviously, you can tell why after hearing these stories. So when I found someone normal, I couldn't help but think that maybe I'd finally caught a break. He made me laugh and we had fun together and that's all I needed to pursue something. We were not dating for almost two months, which was a really good run for me.

He did sweet little things here and there, like drawing a smiley face on my hand before I'd leave so that I'd think of him while I was driving back. He had a cake ready with lit candles when I came over late on my birthday after I'd gone out with some friends (we had only been talking for about a week, so my friends, of course, were priority). My point here being that I wasn't a complete fool. He did things to indicate he was interested, and I was finally willing to accept that someone was truly interested that I also liked.

My family and friends are a huge part of my life and I refuse to be one of those people that shuts them out as soon as I find a guy, so oftentimes when I was in town, I also had plans with family or friends. I would invite him to join to include him, but not to force him to meet my family or friends. He would always happily agree and tag along. The most nerve-wracking moment was introducing him to "my boys." My group of extremely close guy friends from high school, who are more protective and judgmental than my brothers. I warned him beforehand all it would take to win approval was buying them drinks. He bravely and happily walked into a group of 8 or so terribly critical guys, shook their hands and bought a few pitchers. My boys were happy; I was happy.

It seemed all of my friends and family were pleased. Although in hindsight, I found out they were just pleased that I was happy. Turns out, none of them liked him from the get-go. HUGE RED FLAG. If family and friends are willing to be honest and let you know that they don't like the person you are dating, RUN! The people in your life that mean the most to you indicate what kind of person you are. If those same people can't see this new person fitting into your life, then what's the point? Granted, it takes them telling you in order for you to be aware of it, which is usually the problem, but still.

There I was, happy, willing to jump in, so out of character for me, but I was okay with it. He wasn't as eager, but he went about it in such a way that I didn't realize it for a while. I guess he was in a pretty serious relationship with the girl he dated before me. I was a cool girl, though, and didn't mind, so it didn't matter. Except it did. She still called him, still *needed* him, they still shared cell phone bills and friends.

One night, I noticed a book on his desk about how to pick out an engagement ring. They had only been broken up for about a month or two, so he still had some unresolved emotions to work through. I should have run then, but I was happy. I didn't want there to already be a reason for this not to work, especially because when it was good, it was really good.

I never ask for the label of girlfriend, but I can't say I'm not insulted that I've never had it. Still, I never tried to initiate that talk, but he would go out of his way to make it clear that we weren't going to label it. This was insulting, and I again should've run then, but I still wanted to believe he was just working through his issues and just needed time. That's how he would explain it, he just needed time, but he really did like me. Normally, in my right mind, I would've been like "Bye! I'll find someone who doesn't need time to know they want to be with me." For whatever reason, though, I was caught up in this thing, whatever it was. I think I wanted to believe I was capable of opening and letting someone in, or wanted to believe that someone could want me (*tragic, I know*) so I powered on.

Ultimately, he continued to pull away and I got more frustrated with him every day. A few signs started standing out to me that this wasn't as great as I thought. First, he didn't really like my dog and my dog didn't care for him. This sounds silly, but I'm such a dog person and my dog is practically a child to me, so I really need a man who loves my dog. Not to mention that dogs are generally good judges of character. I'm just saying. She knew. She told me long before my family and friends did.

The second was a huge sign that somehow went undetected for a while, but once I noticed, it hit me like a brick wall. As previously stated, music is my passion. For some reason, he was always in charge of the music. I could play music if I was driving, but he would freely change it until he'd hear something he wanted to hear. When I tried to listen to my favorite singer in the car, he would change the song. I can't even begin to describe how offensive I find this. I would put it back on, and he changed it again and said we weren't listening to it. He hadn't even heard it, so I'm not sure why he was so adamantly against it. Not to mention, if he did dislike it, there are certain sacrifices you make, and listening to a song you don't like is a tiny compromise to make. Get over it and listen to the damn three-minute song. Little things like this indicate what kind of person someone is. It was becoming clear to me that he was a selfish narcissist, who was not kind or giving. This just happened to be a small indicator of his true character. Respect is one of the qualities I'm searching for, and this was a clear sign that it was something he didn't possess.

Along the same lines, he didn't like *concert me.* My favorite pastime is going to see concerts, so he really needed to be on board with it. I'm not sure why (probably ex-girlfriend baggage), but it really bothered him that I wanted to be up front and singing and dancing along with friends. *Guess what, fool? None of my friends' guys like it—but they either suck it up and do it, or find a spot a little further back to gather and enjoy it on their terms.* He was always super whiney when things didn't go his way, which is a terrible quality in a child—let alone an adult.

He then proceeded to have another conversation about spending time with my family and how it felt like we were rushing things. Nobody told him he had to go, so I don't know why he was complaining. If it felt too fast, say it before you meet them, dumbass.

The final straw was at the rodeo one night. We were going to see Zac Brown Band. I rode in with two of his friends from College Station, and we had to stop on our way for them to pick something up. We were running late because of it, and I didn't get a chance to meet up with any of my friends while there (because his friends always took priority). He showed no affection and hardly any acknowledgment of my presence. It almost seemed as if it was an inconvenience that I was there.

Needless to say, I had finally had enough. He was clearly pushing me away, but was too much of a coward to end it himself. So I thought I'd pull together my pride and hold steady to my history of not getting my heart broken. Although it hurt like hell, I was strong (motivating myself with John Mayer "Say What You Need to Say" on repeat) and ultimately said what I needed to say. He, of course, wasn't surprised, and had his apologies ready. I made it clear I was done being strung along, and we parted ways.

The most annoying part of all of this was a few months later I found out he told people we both decided it wasn't working out. *Um, no— you jackass, you acted like a baby and waited for me to end it. I get bragging rights on dumping you. Thanks, bye!*

We parted as *friends* because we would go on to still work game days together, but luckily football season ended and I didn't have to see him for a while. I was pretty bummed for a few weeks. My car rides were filled with crying and passionately singing along to Taylor Swift *Last Kiss* and

Colbie Caillat *I Never Told You*—Turns out I become a basic bitch during a breakup (if you can even call it that if they were never your boyfriend), but hey—what can I say? Music is my everything, and I definitely need it for expressing my feelings and healing. As my life's song says: *She's got a handful of records that she turns to when she needs to land.*

I began to break through and see all of the red flags for what they were. I eventually found peace and strength in ending it. I was happy before I had to see him again, and when I did, he was introducing me to his new girlfriend. His "best friend" while we were dating, the one that I almost felt threatened by, but figured the bigger issue was the girl from the past. He's now engaged to that girl. For some reason, a terrible pattern developed somewhere along the way where as soon as me and a guy were done, they ended up marrying the next girl they dated. Another cool ego boost for me. Anyway, all I knew at the time was that it wasn't right, and I'm glad I was brave enough to end it before he screwed me around anymore.

In the last few months, I've realized how much I admire strength. I realized that in order to become someone I could really be proud of, I needed to figure out what trait I admired most in others, and become that. Through years of idolizing my mother and just recently finding inspiring woman that guide my way, what I've come to find is that I think one of the most beautiful things a woman can be is strong. Now every day, I fight to be just that.

I wish I could be proud of myself in all of these chapters, but unfortunately when writing a book you are forced to see yourself clearly when you may have tried to block it out of your memory because you weren't always that great. Looking back on stories like this, I'm ridiculously proud that I could be strong through all of other people's craziness, without even realizing that's what I longed to be more than anything else.

Chapter 5

The Projects

"Always there every time you need me; it ain't love, but just like nicotine, you're addicted to a feeling you can only get from me and your cigarettes."
Miranda Lambert, *Me and Your Cigarettes*

Settle in my friends, this could be a long one…

I'm not sure which is worse, my chronic attraction to men who are "projects" or the fact that as I mapped out chapters for this book, I almost didn't procure a place for them. Obviously one day I'll discuss this with a therapist and find out what deep-seeded issues are in play here, but for now I can only hypothesize: Perhaps it has something to do with my own personal sense of feeling damaged, and the desire to help someone else who feels broken find a way to feel whole again. I'm more concerned with the possibility that it stems from my desire to be in control of things, or the idea that if I can bring someone joy by "fixing" their feeling damaged, that they'll be destined to love me. Or worst of all, maybe it's simply my insecurities surfacing, and that I feel broken in a way that no one who is entirely "whole" will be able to love me.

Whatever the reason, there is unfortunately something so damn attractive about a man who has a secret dark and broken side. As I write these words, I understand how disturbing that sounds, but I suppose I try not to see it that way. You see, I've always found "the wrong guy" attractive. The broken and damaged Chuck Bass, the dark and twisted Alex Karev, and the abandoned and unloved Shawn Hunter of the fiction world are the characters I always pull for to find their way and win the girl. I can't help but see the sexiness of the dark. However, ultimately the lesson here is that in the light of day, there is nothing attractive about someone who feels inadequate and still needs to find their own happiness before they can truly love someone else. No matter how right you are for them or how whole you can make them feel, they are still incomplete, and can only become whole on their own terms through their own work. They are sad and lost, and that shouldn't be capitalized on any more than a desperate, insecure girl who gets taken advantage of by some arrogant guy. It's just not a healthy base for any relationship, and my dysfunctional attraction to it is entirely problematic.

I spent years on one such project, and unhealthy is an understatement for whatever our connection was or wasn't. I truly believed in him and saw in him the man he could never see in himself. I saw a heart of gold in this tortured soul, and wanted to believe that I could be the one who made him see the light. I hoped I could be the reason he wanted to let that version of himself shine. Oh, how naïve I was.

It all began the summer after I went off to college. My friends and I were all back home for three months and made the absolute most of our time together. We picked up right where we left off, and we were pretty much free of responsibility. Those few months were spent practically living in the backyard of our friend Cody's house. Whether poolside during the day or beer pong by night, you'd find us all gathered around that glass table and wooden porch swing, laughing and soaking up the summer memories we'd reminisce on for years to come.

My project had practically grown up in that house, as he'd struggled with family issues and was taken in by Cody's family (he and Cody's older brother were always close friends). Since he was a few years older, I hadn't really known him before that summer, but by the end we were really something. All it would take was a backyard, a guitar, and a lake house paradise.

***

Due to my obsession with music, I've always had a thing for musicians. I can't fight it. There's something about that poet soul that makes me feel an instant connection. I've always been a writer and completely inspired by lyrics, but have never been musically gifted. I am in awe of anyone who can take the writing piece, which is so difficult within itself, and combine it with the impossible talent of creating music.

Well, I'll be damned if my project wasn't a backyard musician, who strummed my heart strings like he did that worn out old guitar. He had the most beautiful raspy voice, and I could listen to him sing for hours. Twisted and tragic lyrics were his specialty and my kryptonite. It only took a few nights of group sing-alongs and after-hours serenades for me to fall quickly.

Being the guys' girl that I am, I was always up late, hanging with the best of them. I was one of the last of my friends to take to drinking, but once I embraced it, I really harnessed my competitive nature in with it, and quickly became the girl who could drink any guy under the table. In college, it was something I could really pride myself on, though my mom always saw it as a terrible disappointment. Either way, I really could hang. There we would be, 3:30 AM in Cody's backyard, the last three or four of us, refusing to be the next one to give up and go to bed. As the numbers dwindled down, so did the ability to make good choices, and the coupling off ensued. My project and I would be on the swing, chatting through an in-depth conversation, with me continuously probing him for more details on his dark and trying childhood or his past long-term relationship that ended poorly. The psychiatrist in me can't help myself; I just need people to talk through all of it, so that they can come to find the clarity they need. It only gets worse when I drink because I'm convinced I can solve the world's problems.

We would talk through all of his issues, allowing him to see that I *understand* what he's going through and am fully supportive. He opened up to me, which made me feel valued. (*Gag*, can I go back and punch myself in the face?) It didn't take long for us to feel the immediate connection, or maybe it was the rum? Whatever it was, we were hooked.

A few more nights spent with him playing songs he'd written and he'd taken a wrecking ball to the walls I kept up around me. It was like taking a magnifying glass to his soul and I couldn't keep my lips off of his. Despite his disgusting and repulsive habit of smoking (which I'm never ok with, but made the exception for him), I enjoyed kissing him more than anyone else I had kissed—which was a lot. I still and will forever hate smoking with a burning passion (pun intended), but I loved kissing him so much, I grew fond of the faintest hint of cigarette smoke mixed with whiskey, which he always tasted of. I began to crave it, which is why this disaster went on and off for years.

Here's another issue: when you are enamored with someone who you are trying to fix, you find yourself trying to change them, which is another thing I swore I'd never do. My mom always told me never to plan on changing a man and that the things you fight about or don't like when you are dating are the things you'll fight about forever once you are married. I understood these pieces of advice well, and never intended to be the kind of girl who wanted to change someone. After all, you're supposed to love each other for who you are, right? Only, it's never that simple. When you finally find someone you adore, you want to find a way to make it work. Since I was already subconsciously working on him as a project, I convinced myself smoking was a part of what he needed fixed. I decided it was one of the things he wanted to make better in his life. I believed it so much that I would take the cigarette out of his mouth before he could light it and break it in half. I'd then sheepishly smile, as if my being adorable would hide the fact that I was basically tearing his money in half and throwing it on the ground. He didn't seem that mad, as he would replace the cigarette, and the whole thing would start over. Why he kept letting it happen, I'll never understand, but I just kept doing it. He wasn't pleased, but ultimately he wasn't angry with me and I got to kiss him without the taste of smoke in our mouths. I felt it was a small victory, but again, you can't have any intention of changing someone to be what you need them to be. Therefore, this ultimately only added to the toxicity between us.

The main red flag to make note of here is that if you feel the need to *FIX* or *CHANGE* someone, it's not ever going to be right. If you can't accept and forgive their flaws, it will never work. It's one thing to bring out the best in each other or feel a desire to be better for the person you're with, it's an entirely different thing, however, to *expect* someone to be a better version of their self for you. Especially if you're taking such personal stakes in their success at changing, you'll only be let down and let each other down.

***

Fast forward a few weeks in, when we started in on our regular weekend trips to the paradise lake house. Every other weekend, we'd pile into our cars, loaded down with beer, snacks, and good tunes. We'd head north to the lake for three days of fun, sun, and young love. This lake house had been our refuge for years, and that summer was absolute perfection. It was the last time we'd all get to spend that much time together, and we made sure each and every trip was the best weekend ever. I can't help but think it was no coincidence that this Kid Rock song came out that summer:

> *Catching Walleye from the dock*
> *Watching the waves roll off the rocks*
> *She'll forever hold a spot inside my soul*
> *We'd blister in the sun, we couldn't wait for night to come*
> *To hit that sand and play some rock 'n' roll*
>
> *While we were trying different things*
> *And we were smoking funny things*
> *Making love out by the lake to our favorite song*
> *Sipping whiskey out the bottle, not thinking 'bout tomorrow*

My favorite part of every lake trip was any night we built a fire. We would all circle up around the small fire pit in flimsy plastic chairs, our faces illuminated by the lambent flames. I'm not sure which was more radiant, the flicker of blue and orange we sat around or the spark in my eye as my project plucked along to songs we all knew. We sang along and swayed in the glow of night, our echoes trailing off into the night, as unadulterated happiness filled our hearts. A few songs in, and someone else would take over the guitar, leaving the lap of luxury open for me. We'd snuggle in pure bliss until the crappy piece of plastic would crumble below us, leaving everyone in laughter. It was hard to fight these feelings, when it was all so pure and well-intended. In fact, throughout all the nights we spent together, we almost never exceeded first base. It was always passionate, but more about the emotional connection than anything.

In hindsight, it all sounds so idyllic. However, neither of our intentions were as pure as I may pretend to recall. One obvious issue being that I went into it all hoping to be the reason he'd want to be better. The other main issue being that he had no intention of changing, just wanted to party, and had no plan of anything serious ever developing (even if I'd like to believe he did, but didn't know how). If this is not a recipe for disaster, I really don't know what is.

We went on like this, back and forth over the span of about three years. We never talked except when we were together and drinking (RED FLAG, duh!) Obviously, this ultimately led to nothing. I never even really got any closure. We just always seemed to fade away: with the end of summer, the end of a weekend, or the end of a night. I was too cool to bring up wanting anything more, and he was too emotionally closed off to consider the idea. It's for the best, I suppose, as he truly needed to work through his crap without me.

He went on to seriously date a couple more girls, one of which was maybe the dumbest human ever. He was with her for almost a year, and he pushed away everyone is his life for her. Again I will repeat: If everyone in your life doesn't like the person you are dating, RUN LIKE HELL. Run like they are literally trying to kill you. She told a room full of adults and teachers that the last book she'd read was Hop On Pop in first grade, never brought anything to contribute to a social gathering, acted like a child/treated my project like a child, argued with him at least twice daily, and basically undid everything I worked hard on for years in developing his self-esteem. Thanks a lot, bitch.

The next girl he dated was normal and kind. She's a little older, and seems good for him. They're now engaged. I really do hope the best for him, and I know that we were never right for each other. I just hope that the current girl is not sitting in the same situation I sat in for years, working on fixing him. If only I could've tattooed him in a way that she would know what to expect. Although, the barbed-wire Texas tattoo on his ass should have been sign enough for both of us…

Chapter 6

The Neighbor

"Hey boy, don't you know I got something going on. All my friends are gonna come gonna party all night long… So boy won't you come?"
Christina Aguilera, Come On Over

Moving right along to the apartment neighbor situation. Mine just happened to be in college and we had a couple of different sets of neighbors. Now, let's be honest, the obvious appeal here is the convenience factor, and the simplicity of the meet cute. Although, I will warn that it seems so simplistic that you may just orchestrate one yourself, and this makes it less cute. In my case, there were two sets of neighbors in particular with whom I did just that.

My sophomore year of college, I was living with Chad, who I basically grew up with (our moms are best friends). Yes, the same Chad as Thursday Night wingman. We had just recently moved in to our first apartment, me fresh out of the dorms and Chad straight (no pun intended) out of his mom's house. We were on our own and so excited to have an apartment of our very own. We realized quickly that there were two guys living next door to us, who were slightly older and quite attractive. I was pretty sure at the time that they played football. I still to this day don't know if that was true or not, but let's pretend they did. I was always hoping to run into them, just catching a glimpse here and there.

Finally, one night, after my friends had heard me talk about them for weeks, Hillary and Jen were there to witness them from the balcony as they arrived home one evening. Hillary got the bold idea that we would go over and ask them if we could borrow something, the classic neighbor story. We weren't sure yet what that would be, but we were sure it was our only option, so we sat around brainstorming. We had to come up with something that wasn't weird to ask for, something they would probably have, and something that made us seem like we were being relatively normal on a Thursday night (not sitting around creeping on our neighbors). For some unknown reason, we came up with orange juice. She poured vodka in a cup and decided we could tell them that we started to make drinks and then realized that we were out of orange juice (*idiots*). Then, even more ridiculous, the three of us decided to walk over there together with one cup of vodka (*so fucking stupid*). One roommate answered the door, we then proceeded to ask if they can help us out with our dilemma, nearly in unison (*seriously, what were we thinking?*). The one roommate gets the other to grab the orange juice, they pour some in our cup and we were convinced we nailed it.

Of course, we reminisced on this over the next few days, and realized just how stupid it all was. Thinking back on it, the look on their faces was pure bewilderment, and we had to look like such idiots. We never talked to them again. They moved a few months later (hopefully not because of us).

The next neighbors who moved in were not as cute, but they were pretty good looking. One of them was a little short for my taste, but the other was cute and right up my alley (say it with me now, *tall*). However, I had learned my lesson with neighbors, and had no intention of getting my hopes up.

A couple of months after they had been living there, it was Christmas time. Many people left on Christmas break, but I was still working for a week or two after we got done with finals. Upon taking my dog out for a walk one day, I noticed a package outside their door. The next day, I noticed it was still there. The parking lot was pretty empty and I hadn't remembered seeing either of their cars recently (not a stalker, just observant), so I start to think maybe he left on Christmas break and this would be sitting here for weeks. I decided I would keep an eye on it, and if it was still there at the end of the week, I'd take it in with me so that no one would steal it. At that point, I was legitimately being a courteous neighbor, with no intention of being a creeper.

The end of the week rolled around, the box was still there, and the neighbors' cars still were not. I took the box in, and by that time, I was leaving soon to head home for the holidays. I thought it would be kind of weird if he did come back and was waiting on something and it was gone, so I decided to let him know it wasn't stolen. Instead of leaving a note on the door like a normal human, I found the name on the box, looked him up on Facebook and sent him a message. I noticed it was the cute, tall one, and in that moment, it probably became weird and stalker-ish. I composed as normal of a message I could come up with:

Hey, this may sound weird, but I noticed you had a box delivered, and it was out there for several days. I figured you guys left for Christmas break, so I brought it in to my apartment so that no one would steal it. Let me know when you're back in town and I'll bring it over.

He responded pretty quickly, and was extremely thankful. He said it was a Christmas gift from his grandfather, and it was supposed to have arrived before he left. He said that he really appreciated me taking it in and letting him know.

Upon his return, he sent another message with his number and said whenever it was convenient for me that he would come pick it up. We worked out a time, and he promptly knocked at my door. We casually made small talk as I handed it over. He again expressed his gratitude and explained that it was an irreplaceable gift, and he had been very worried about it.

From that day, we greeted each other warmly and encountered each other often. We started inviting each other and accompanying roommates when we'd have people over. We usually had previous plans, but eventually got around to actually hanging out from time to time. One night, I came home from a night out with friends and took my dog out for a walk. I walked by in view of their balcony (not on purpose, it just happened to be my route), and I still looked good from my night out. He and his roommate and a couple of friends were still up drinking and listening to music. They invited me to join them. I played it cool, took my dog back home, and arrived at their door a little while later. I brought over a beer of my own from home, with the intention of just drinking that and returning home. He and I got to talking out on the balcony (what is it with those things??). He offered another beer; we ended up hitting it off, chatted a little while longer, he went for the goodnight kiss, and called it a night.

I only had to walk twelve steps home! Again, this convenience is the draw of "The Neighbor." Lonely or bored—they are right next door. After party drinks – you are right next door, no driving required. Feeling pretty – walk by their patio and get yourself a compliment. Win, win, win.

Though the convenience is appealing, it more than likely turns into nothing. You also hold the convenience factor to him. Bring some friends over or have a hot roommate, they'll work too. A new neighbor moves in, and either of you are more than willing to be the first to jump ship and check out the new neighbors.

I brought a couple of friends over there one night and he was out on the balcony making out with one of them. No real feelings ever were involved for him and I; so who really cares? Just be aware of what you are getting yourself into and the potential for future awkward encounters. After all, leases are binding, people.

Chapter 7

The Best Friend / Future Husband

"Anything other than yes is no, anything other than staying's going,
anything less than I love you is lying."
John Mayer, *Friends, Lovers, or Nothing*

This was a situation I knew all too well in high school, that trickled down through college and into parts of my adult life. Tragically I must admit that for whatever reason, I have come across very few guys who are initially interested in me. When Mom wants to know why I can't find anyone, I really don't know what to tell her beyond the fact that there is little interest and that I hardly meet anyone that is available anyway. I'm pretty sure that I'm not super ugly or annoying, so I don't know exactly what the deal is. All I know is that it's not until a guy really gets to know me that he becomes interested in/ attracted to me. This leads to excessive numbers of "best friend" guys in my life. They get to know me, and then decide I'm this really cool laid back girl who can hang out with "the guys." *Great, thanks.*

Don't get me wrong; I am completely grateful for every one of those friendships. I've never been a real girl's girl, and needed/ loved these friendships. However, it's incredibly frustrating to be habitually single and constantly hear from guys how great you are. After a while, you're left thinking *"Ummm helloo?! Can someone give me some constructive feedback here and tell me what the actual issue is*?" But they don't. High school was when this was most confusing for me because those same best friends were the ones I'd end up drunk and making out with. Again, not complaining, but damn. I don't get it. You tell me I'm awesome always; you're attracted enough to make out with me; what's the problem? Cut to them having girlfriend after crazy girlfriend and then complaining to me about these "crazy bitches." Well I don't know what to tell you, fools. I'm not crazy, but you don't want my non-crazy ass, so I can't help you. It seemed to me that they were purposely chasing the crazy. (We saw signs of this before in chapter 3.) I just find this humorous because any self-help books I've encountered are all directed at women and how to fix themselves, when in reality, through my own extensive research, I've come to find it usually comes down to guys chasing the crazy, and women shouldn't have to play games to pretend to be exactly what these guys are wanting. The guys have their own issues, but are unwilling to believe in the concept of self-help, so their books don't exist.

I also always thought it was a good thing that I started out friends with guys. Relationships should be built on friendships, and I thought, "Well why not?" It makes perfect sense, especially if these guys are the ones that are able to see the true me and like me for who I am.

My point here is that there were plenty of almosts for me. Guys that I thought if I just keep on being me, one day they will wake up and realize it just made sense. There were two in particular that I really thought would end up being something for real. Both of which made "backup" deals with me—*If we are still single at 30, we will marry each other.* Spoiler alert: I'm now 27 and both are married... not to me. I know you're shocked. Try to contain it. Of course at this point in my life, I realize it wasn't meant to be with either of them, but the high school/college version of me never understood what the issue was. There was so much chemistry there, and attraction and friendship. What was missing? I guess I still don't really know, but I know that if it was meant to be it would've happened a long time ago. They would be the ones to bring it up. It was all so comfortable and easy to the point that they could talk about us ending up with each other forever, but not enough to date me right then? This was exhausting and disheartening to my eighteen/nineteen year old self who just didn't get it. While I'm completely happy for them, and I understand it never would have really worked out because they were looking for something else (tiny blondes like everyone else seems to be looking for), it still is sometimes tough to think back and still be unclear of what the problem was. At the end of the day, it's much easier to blame them than to try to think if there's anything I could have done differently, especially since I really don't think there was. It just really isn't fair and if guys thought half as much as women do about things like this, maybe they'd think twice before saying some of this *forever* bullshit to someone they aren't actually interested in.

On the flip side of this, there was another close friend that I dated for a few weeks (the original of the same names). In that case, I really adored him and he made me feel really great about myself. He was so sweet and cute, but for some reason the attraction just wasn't there like I wanted it to be. He's one of those truly great guys, but it just wasn't going to work out. It really bums me out because he to this day is one of the best humans I've ever known in my life. We are still really great friends, and I want nothing but the best for him. He's found a really great girl now too, and it's great to see how it can all work out for the best. I hope I never led him on like the other guys did to me, but I guess I can see how it's hard if you want something to work out, but you just can't force it. I really am grateful to him for always seeing the best in me and reminding me to see it too. He still has to be my therapist for me sometimes when we get to drinking and I'm feeling lonely. He puts up with a lot of my complaining and reminds me to just keep on trucking. He is the kind of guy best friend friend you actually want.

I had another guy best friend that I adored. We knew each other since Kindergarten. Seriously. We became extremely close in high school and really were best friends. He was always dating someone. I was obviously always dating no one, but we could talk about anything and were always there for each other. We could pick each other up when we were down and hold each other when we felt lonely. It was a really good deal we had. We made the same backup marriage deal. The only issues started when one of us would develop real feelings for the other and wish it was more. The timing of it all never worked out, and we both just ended up feeling sad for different periods of time in there, as we traded off back and forth when we would have feelings for each other. By the end of senior year, we were back to being great friends and he invited me to prom. We had an absolute blast, and he ended up sleeping with three girls that weekend (happy to report none of them were me). Seriously. Just because I didn't plan on sleeping with you doesn't mean you have to embarrass me by sleeping with three of my friends in one weekend. Even these awesome "best friends" will let you down and hurt your feelings in ways you never thought they would. Obviously, that relationship was going nowhere. We tried to stay friends, but between college and moving away, it just kind of faded over time. He just recently bought a house and moved in with his girlfriend, so I think the ship has sailed on that backup deal as well.

But really who wants to be someone's backup? You're supposed to end up in a relationship where both of you feel like you got the better deal, not one where you both feel like you lost a bet. It makes me sad to think I have always been so sure I'd end up alone that I felt the need to make three backup marriage plans (I think there were more along the way). Although, in all actuality, I may have been on to something seeing where I am now, but again I'd still rather hold out hope that there's someone out there interested enough in the great person I am to choose me. It just sucks because it seems like this cycle continues. I still have countless close guy friends. There are a few single guys here and there in my life that I feel like I have great chemistry with and again there is attraction on my end, but I'm still somehow always the friend. I wonder if it even crosses their minds to have any kind of interest in me or if I am just some asexual figure that hangs out and is fun to be around and isn't annoying/crazy so I just automatically enter the friend zone without consideration. *Heavy sigh, eye roll, and just keep movin' on…*

Chapter 8

The Almost Lover

"It must have been love, but it's over now..."
Roxette, *Must Have Been Love*

Maybe it was love, maybe it wasn't, but either way it's over now. And when something is over, it should stay over.

Never having been in a serious relationship, I've never really been in love or had to say those words to anyone. I came close at one point, I think someone almost said it to me on the phone around the same time I was ready to end things. I awkwardly acted distracted by something and quickly changed the subject and had to wait until the next phone call to end things to make it a little less awkward.

However, there was one guy that I look back on and think he was probably the closest I came to real feelings. He's quite a bit older, and I knew him from a very young age. He's from a small town where our family has a farm, and he's friends with my older cousins. Once I was older, we found an attraction that we couldn't fight. It was kept a secret from the family at first, but eventually couldn't be kept hidden. I was in college at the time and he was living three and half hours from me, so it wasn't in the cards, but we kind of just went for it anyway. I was still so young, and inexperienced with relationships. I wasn't ready for what he was ready for, and if timing had been a little different, the whole thing may have turned out differently. However, as we all know timing is more than half the battle and it just wasn't right for us. I went to visit him a few times, and he came to visit me once or twice. It just became completely evident what different places we were in when we would visit each other's respective lives. I couldn't drink legally, so meeting him and his friends somewhere was uncomfortable and I just felt judged and extremely young. When he came to visit my little college town, he couldn't stay with me because I was still in a dorm. We were living in two completely different worlds and despite the amazing connection we had, it was just a little more than I was ready to deal with. We were kind of crazy about each other, but let it die down and moved on with our lives. He started seeing someone else, and I was secretly jealous. I had no right to be, as I had my chance and missed out. So I moped about it a little and decided he was the one I let get away.

A few months later, we saw each other at a party at my cousin's. Of course there was drinking involved and what started as cordial pleasantries and mostly ignoring each other, turned into the need for closure and a drunken conversation about what exactly went wrong. I confessed to him that I handled it poorly because I was overwhelmed and didn't know what else to do and that I was sorry about it because I really did care about him and couldn't believe I let him get away. He then decided that he wanted me this whole time too and was hoping I'd come to that very revelation. He offered to drive me back to my farm (something that was unnecessary as I could have walked, which would have been a much better choice). As most rides home do, it turned into an out of the way route where the car was parked and we had more to say. Ultimately, he started to kiss me. I stopped him to remind him that he had someone else now, to which his response was, "Yeah, but she's not you..." Why I allowed it, I don't know, but I went along with it for a few minutes until he eventually took me home. Someone should slap 19-year-old me in the face. What a dumb response. Him reverting back to me once it's over and while he's with someone else is not cute and flattering, it's infidelity in the making.

Obviously nothing more became of that. In fact, I didn't hear from him again for a very long time after that. He stayed with that girl for a while and then things didn't work out. He has since found someone else, gotten married, and moved down the street from me. So that's just great. Even though he may have been the closest thing to love and a real relationship I'd ever known, when things don't work out, it's not just going to magically fix itself over one drunken conversation.

What's in the past should stay in the past; there's a reason it was there in the first place, just leave it there. Returning to something old is more than likely not a good idea. People tend to go back because it's comfortable, easy, or they're lonely. We tend to "forget" the things that put it in the past in the first place, and pretend we can go back to it. It's just not a good idea.

This situation is not too far off from the drunken phone calls and texts you (or I) receive from people who are just having a shitty lonely night and need some company (or sex). Alcohol really makes relationships much more of a shit show than they already are. Tread lightly people, and turn off your phone. Or just go to bed. Dragging things back up from the past is never a good idea. If someone tells you otherwise, they are the exception and shouldn't be counted on for advice at two in the morning. I don't know how many times we all have to learn this lesson. I'm always brought back to this Wade Bowen song lyric when it comes to things like this:

"Is there any way to learn from what you've been told or do you really have to hold the experience?"

We know better. We've been told time and time again. We've seen other people go through it, but for some reason we just have to put ourselves through it anyway to be sure we aren't the exception to some unspoken rule. We sometimes want to believe that this lesson to be learned doesn't apply to us and we can live it better and differently than those before us. I'm pretty sure we would be much better off if we just assumed we weren't the exception and didn't bother, but this is coming from someone who had to hold the experience and has already been there and done that because I couldn't take anyone's word for it. Don't fall back into something old because it's easy or comfortable, there's a reason it didn't work. Definitely don't find yourself involved with cheating, in your relationship or in someone else's.

I know my main goal here is to tell you to laugh at love, but sometimes it just isn't all that funny. This was one of those cases, and all you can do is move on to the next chapter in life (*and in this book because it's a good one!*)

Editor's Note:

My editor would like me to add a disclaimer here to inform readers that I may not be giving sound advice in this chapter. She was in a relationship that ended for a couple of years, but they ultimately got back together and are now happily married. As it turns out, all of my advice in this book may only apply to my life. So if you're reading this thinking I'm critical and cynical and you aren't going to listen to anything I say, I guess I can't really argue with you there. As long as you are able to laugh at love, I support your choices. Except the cheating thing, that one seems like fair advice that we should all agree to abide by.

Chapter 9

The Beach Boys

"He showed off, splashing around... Summer sun, something's begun, but oh, oh these summer nights."
Grease, *Summer Nights*

Just as in previous chapters, there can be many variations of the readily available "beach boys." In my case I encountered these far more often than I needed to.

My first experience with said beach boys actually dates back to my junior year of high school. I went to Destin with my friend Kelsie's family. We met two guys who were brothers, who were just "like soo hot." They were on vacation with their family as well, but were slightly older than us. We had wandered off on our own for a walk down the beach, obviously to see if we'd meet any cute boys. We did just that, as they were on a walk of their own. As it turned out, they happened to only be staying a few houses down from us. Convenient. We made plans to meet up with them later on in the night. After bargaining with Kelsie's parents, we were able to get an hour of freedom if we showed them where we'd be and agreed that parents would be there. We walked down to their place, and much to our surprise they had forgone dinner with their family, so it was just us and these guys. They were mostly awful. They immediately insisted on coupling off and separating us. We went ahead and immediately disagreed to that, and just hung out as a group for a while. They did cannon balls into the pool as if they were 7, while we watched and laughed, and whispered about how cute they were.

After all the pool fun wore off, they decided again that it was time for separation. Turns out, they were all about forcing things. We noticed that fact once they separated us and used the same forceful routine on both of us. We compared notes later and both had forcefully kissed us, tried to force us to touch their penises, and got upset when we weren't willing to have sex with them. In the end, we didn't need the full hour we were granted and returned home laughing about their unfortunate kissing skills and forceful tactics.

I think the biggest problem with beach boy situations is the sheer paradox of men versus women's expectations. To women, the beach is a hopeful, romantic place with wind and waves and sunsets: it's like a freaking episode of The Bachelor. While on the other hand, because women see it this way, the beach just makes guys horny and expectant. Sure they'll do a little hand holding and beach walking, but only if it ends with them getting laid.

As I got older, so did the beach boys and the evolution was transparent and obvious. Take the scene from high school, add alcohol and subtract parental supervision entirely. Now they aren't only horny, but drunk and horny. So are plenty of the girls. This then adds some truth to guys' expectations, as plenty of girls live out their "Bachelorette" episodes and go straight to the fantasy suite, or throw out all expectations and settle for a little male attention and action on the beach. The guys get lazier as time and alcohol wears on, and less effort is required. Moral of the story: if you have big plans of meeting the man of your dreams while strolling down the beach at sunset, you may want to rethink that.

Now let's be clear, just because you don't necessarily want to end up with these beach boys, you should be aware that they can be a lot of fun. Cut to me and the girls: Spring Break, 2010, Panama City Beach, Florida. Not one of us hooked up with anyone, but dammit if we didn't have the time of our lives with some beach boys next door.

We rolled into PCB, 5 girls and 8 suitcases piled into one car, after an excessively long journey from Texas, with a pit stop night one in New Orleans. We were already off to a rough start, considering the hellish hangovers New Orleans blessed us with before knocking us out and sending us on our way. After some misguided directions and concern that we were lost, we finally found the elusive ABV Inn. Now I'm not sure about America's Best Value, but it was definitely PCB's best value, as it was the cheapest place we could find on the beach. We were quite excited to find that we were only about a mile from party beach, and could walk back if it was completely necessary (it never got to that point for us, as a mile walking drunk quickly feels like 8).

We trekked up the stairs, unloading luggage, and starting to clear our hung-over heads with the ocean air. Before we could even unload the last of our luggage, the door next to our room burst open with loud music and half-drunk, half-clothed college guys pouring out into the outdoor hallway to shotgun some beers. Without hesitation, we joined them and began to probe them with questions about the beach. Considering their current state, we had assumed they'd been here longer than us. Well, as turned out, they had only just arrived a half hour before us, so they had none of the answers we needed, but all the alcohol they needed (at least for that day).

It was fairly late in the day, but we weren't that interested in getting all dolled up to go out and spend a crap load of money, only to be hung-over again tomorrow for beach party time. We decided to just drink at our hotel with these beach boys next door. They were in town from Indiana, high school friends reunited, half of which went to Purdue. We taught them Texas drinking things, although for some reason they kept claiming that we were from Texarkana. No one is clear on why, and despite telling them otherwise, they just kept insisting we were "Texarkanies." They taught us drinking things from back home that we never should have learned. They one upped our beer bong with a "paint stick," that we kept thinking they were calling a "pain stick." Our name for it caught on, as that's what it really was— a pain-inflicting stick that literally shot beer down your throat. It was basically a giant syringe that you loaded up with beer and pressed up against the wall until it shot it all in your mouth. These guys were not playing around; they were there for one reason, and one reason only: to get fucked up. We were in full support, as we had a similar plan. It was my only time having a wild PCB spring break, and the other girls were in their senior year about to graduate, so we were all about a good time. They also taught us a couple of songs we had never heard, that they blared on repeat, usually until three or four in the morning: some shit about "Moolah and the Guap," that we quickly changed to "Moolah and the Guac," obviously because they are both green. It just made more sense that way.

We were quick friends with our new neighbors, but drew a hard line upon seeing their disastrous room, that they were not welcome in our room. If they wanted to talk to us, they had to either call our room or knock on the front door. Instead, they insisted on knocking on the connecting door and begging us to unlock it because it would be "so fun!" We endearingly re-named all of them, and they did the same.

It was a good thing we had going. We went off and had our own fun-filled days, and would join back up later on. We went to party beach and got "All the way turnt up..." (our other theme song of the week) in weather that was far too cold to be parading around in bathing suits. Girls shrieked and ran into the water long enough to squat and pee, while guys disgustingly peed down their legs or dug holes in the ground to pee and bury. It was the definition of shit show. While I'm glad I got to go and experience it, I'm thankful it was only the one time. That was enough for me. We really embraced the whole experience while it lasted though. We got on people's shoulders and waved flags, stood on coolers and had dance contests, unintentionally and intentionally wound up with other people's shirts, glasses, pants, and somehow a whole pack of energy drinks that I'm pretty sure no one approved of us taking, which was re-named "Turkey Juice" by the beach boys because of how it looked and tasted. We paid $20 to get into a bar with long lines, dirty dance floors, and shit faced people. We did meet some Jamaican guys who taught us a new dance and that if you say "Bacon" or "Beer Can" with a Jamaican accent, there is no way of knowing the difference. We always wound up back at our hotel and fighting off the boys next door from creeping in our room.

One night, we agreed to go with them to a bar right by our hotel. They were a trip and highly entertaining. We had an absolute blast with them, laughing and dancing. They introduced us to something they called riot punch. They basically just bought a jug of juice, poured half of it out and filled it back up with vodka or rum or both.

At one point, after a "riotous" beach day, we had come back for a much needed shower and nap. Our drunken beach boys, who we had seen out at party beach but refused to drive home, ended up walking back. We heard them come in and start jamming "Moolah and the Guac," and decided to make an exception to our rule and be friendly. The one of us they called "Jackie" opened the door connecting our rooms and jokingly asked them, "Hey, you guys got any roofies or Plan B?" The one we called "Pookie" immediately, without missing a beat, responded with, "Yeah, I have some roofies. Did y'all want some?" We squealed with laughter and horror, tried to slam the door, and let them know this is why we didn't open it before. A couple of them pushed their way in (those pushy beach boys) and planned to apologize for their creepy friend. They were hilarious, drunk, and amusing, but we still kicked them out and told them to return to the other door or phone calls if they needed us. We had refused a few times to take already open drinks, even from our good buddies next door, and thank goodness, knowing now that they really did have a stockpile of roofies. We weren't all that flirty with them, so I'm sure they wouldn't have "wasted" their roofies on us, but damn—You can't trust anyone these days! Obviously, nothing happened with any of these boys on our end, but some poor drunk girls hooked up with these fools, and have their own versions of beach boy stories. Hopefully those stories don't involve roofies, as we've learned how pushy beach boys can be.

To sum things up, Beach Boys are fantastic to have a good time with, just make sure you are clear with yourself on your intentions and expectations before a beach trip. Embrace them and enjoy them for what they are, but you're most likely better off not hooking up with any if you want to remain free of regret and/or STDs. Yes, they are plenty good looking with their sun-kissed skin and beach-ready bodies, but don't be deceived by those overly concealing baseball caps and sunglasses. They probably aren't as great as you are making them out to be. All I'm saying is proceed with caution, and for the love of God, keep your drink covered!

Chapter 10

The Brothers' Friends/Friends' Brothers

"The words are hushed, let's not get busted; just lay entwined here, undiscovered."
Dashboard Confessional, *Hands Down*

Just don't. Don't. No matter how convenient you think it would be, and how life would be so simple if things work out, and what a great story it would be…

Don't.

Chapter 11

The Unforgivable Flaw

"You can tell me when it's over if the high was worth the pain..."
Taylor Swift, *Blank Space*

We all have one. Or more. The unforgiveable flaw. Something you can't get past, no matter who it is. Figure out what that is and stand by it. Don't wait until you find someone, like them and then try to figure out how to overlook it. It doesn't work like that. For anyone. If you know you won't forgive it, don't waste your time or theirs. Don't even get the name of someone who has it.

In my case, I have several. One of which is now a name in itself. In previous chapters, I've discussed several guys who all shared the same name. That name is now off limits. If I meet someone with that name, I seriously turn and walk away. I'm not joking. Ain't nobody got time for that.

Beyond that, there are serious flaws that won't fly with me, and I have stopped even thinking a guy is cute if he possesses that flaw. For example: smoking. Smoking is so repulsive to me, it truly makes me sick to my stomach just being around it. There was a time during my low self-esteem years where I would find myself kissing smokers. Obviously some of "The Projects" were smokers, to the point where I was not only ok with the taste of whiskey and cigarettes in one of their mouths, but that the smell of cigarettes made me miss kissing him, even though it made me physically nauseous. So gross and problematic. I really don't understand how people still smoke. I can maybe understand people who are older who have been smoking all their lives and just never bothered to quit, but I really don't understand people in their 20's and 30's smoking. It is seriously disgusting and everyone has known this for years. One of my favorite things my Crossfit coach ever said during a nutrition seminar was, "Do you guys know people still smoke? It's 2013 and people still smoke. And drink sodas..." While the soda thing may be slightly more understandable, he was truly dumbfounded that people still smoke. I feel the same way. How is it still a thing? Just don't ever start, and then you won't have to worry about quitting; it's that simple.

Some of these unforgivable flaws are unforgivable, not for the flaw in itself, but for what it says about the person. For example, if a guy takes longer to get ready than I do, it is an indication to me that he is more high maintenance than me, and I'm not all about that life. For that reason, I would add it to the list. Note that "All but my boyfriend" was way too high maintenance and took twice as long as me to get ready. What takes you so long? You barely even have hair. Additionally, if family isn't important to a guy, it makes me question their whole set of values. Family is a huge part of my life, and if a guy doesn't feel the same way, we won't ever be on the same page when it comes to priorities. It's a non-negotiable issue that I need someone to understand.

These flaws could be many different things for many different people. For example, a friend of mine was dating a guy who was super into working out and proper nutrition, not a bad thing. However, he refused to eat bread ever. For her, this was a deal breaker. She not only found it completely odd that he never eats it, but she loves it and refuses to deal with that constant battle that she doesn't understand. Another friend's famous slogan was "Bad shoes, bad news." A cute, nice guy could be super interested, but if he had some dirty 90's sketchers on, he had to go.

There are plenty of potential unforgivable flaws out there: bad teeth/breath, piercings, hates dogs (or even worse, likes cats), doesn't like football, etc…

Just know what it is, and avoid it like the plague. Don't waste your time or anyone else's.

Side note: another (un)forgiveable flaw for me is not even really a flaw and can actually be forgiven, but just a trait that I had an issue with. If a guy is shorter than me, I tend to push them away on that quality alone. It means nothing in the long run, but for some reason, I found myself standing firm that it wouldn't work for me. I think I just have always been so insecure about my height (5' 10") and just want to feel like a normal girl who can look up to her man, or feel small in his arms. Yes, I realize that sounds completely anti-feminist, like I want to be tiny and delicate compared to my man. That's not the case. I am still fiercely independent, but for some reason I had strong feelings about it. I feel bad that short guys often get the short (pun intended) end of the stick because most girls prefer tall guys, but then I don't feel that bad because tall girls get screwed over too, because guys prefer short tiny girls. So many tall guys end up with short girls, and it usually pisses me off. However, I just recently have noticed there are some really great short guys out there, and I may have to remove this from my list of flaws because there are far bigger issues to worry about. Point being, stick to the flaws you aren't willing to change on, but like, also, give guys a break for things they can't change that don't really matter.

Chapter 12

The Boring Guy (Too Harsh?)

"Your hearts on the loose, you rolled them sevens with nothing to lose.
This ain't no place for the weary kind."
Ryan Bingham, *The Weary Kind*

Every once in a while, I get a glimmer of hope that the "everything will work out" motto is spot on and I just need to be patient. I finally come across a guy who seems normal, nice, and interested in me enough to actually pursue something. Unfortunately, as I've gotten older, I've become very cautious when I come across someone new with potential. Any slight hesitation I have about them, I end up taking very seriously and keep it in the back of my mind. It's happened a couple of times before, so now I know what to expect. When I get all wrapped up in it and ignore the doubts I'm having, then within a couple of weeks it doesn't work out and I'm left looking like a fool because I rambled on about how great they were, only to now have nothing but negative things to say about them. Maybe you call this cynicism, but for me it's just realism.

In one of these cases, I happened to find a really great guy (of course, so I thought...) and kept the doubts in the back of my mind for future reference.

For this story, we have to venture back again to the Rodeo time of year. It really is a great place to meet people. Whether those people pan out into a relationship is a different story, but still: a great place to meet people. This was a couple of years after the alleged "unicorn" incident, and I had grown much older and wiser. Or perhaps just older. Either way, there we were once again boozing it up and attending the Houston Rodeo. Being that we were older and wiser, we decided to start the day with brunch, as every old and wise woman does. Penny refill mimosas and Mexican food is just not something I'm willing to pass up when someone makes the suggestion. Our drinking adventures began around 11:00 and we enjoyed approximately 13 cents worth of refills each before leaving brunch and Ubering to the Rodeo around 2:30. Strong start, ladies. Very wise.

Once we arrived, we were in hustle mode because we stayed longer than we were supposed to at brunch and therefore had to rush up to our seats. Meagan had an epiphany and remembered that her dad was on the club level and could probably get us in there. That would save us three extra rows of ramps to run up and get us into the club level bars. He met us promptly at the entry of that level, and instead of heading to seats, we headed straight for the bar, where endless options of $5 premium drinks are offered to us, bought for us, and consumed quickly.

Crown and Sprite, Crown and Sprite, Crown and Sprite. Repeat.

The Rodeo events bustled across the TV screen displays around us and we'd catch bits of it, but mostly we were social butterflies enjoying the club level atmosphere. All of the events we "couldn't wait to see" just hours earlier quickly took a back seat to the people-watching entertainment. People- watching then turned into man-hunting for me, which eventually became a game of "I want that one…" This is a very enjoyable game in which an excellent married friend (Meagan) offers to help you get exactly what you want. The rules are very simple and exactly how they sound. You point to a cute passer-by, noting "I want that one." Said married friend then shuffles over to them and prompts them to come join us. The first few attempts that day were failures, as they held up their hand to her to show that they were, in fact, also married. But it didn't take long, and I noticed a very tall, cute guy far across the way. Meagan nearly had to take off in a sprint to catch him, but she did. A quick "Are you here with anyone? Come meet my tall, cute friend," and there he was. Extremely tall, super nice, and had booklets full of drink tickets, which he used to support what had become our problematic (?) drinking habit.

It was around this time where my memory began to grow extremely fuzzy. *I know, I know, drunk again. No need for judgement, just keep reading.* The concert part of the Rodeo began, and we stayed at the bar, watching on the TVs. We chatted with this new guy for quite a while. We were all in agreement that we liked him. He seemed nice and normal, so we continued to hang out with him, and eventually made plans to hang out with him afterward at some kind of after event in the club level of another building. At this point, it is a complete hazy blur of drinks and dancing. I'm pretty sure I even slipped and fell on the dance floor at some point, a real classy lady.

Somehow, I managed to end up separated from my two girls and my purse and phone. Never a situation you want to be in (nor one your friends want you or them to be in). They waited for me and looked for me for much longer than they cared to. When I finally used his phone to call them, they were less than pleased and headed to wait in the taxi line. I had made it onto the light-rail train with this guy, headed back to Midtown with the intention of going out and continuing to drink. One million stops later, I was exhausted. We walked to CVS, apparently got a bottle of wine and "Gone Girl" to watch on Netflix, neither of which was utilized that night. When we walked to his place, I drunkenly helped myself to yet another Crown drink, instead of the wine, and stayed the night there. When it came down to it, I think I judged him a little for not judging me for how drunk I was and still wanting to hang out with me again.

The next morning, he seemed taken aback when I asked if he would take me home. He quickly said, "Of course," as if it shouldn't have to be a question (it shouldn't). He took me home, kissed me goodbye, and texted again later that day. All the right things. Greeting my friends was less pleasant. I'm fairly certain neither of them talked to me for about a week after this. Fair, but I really don't even know how it all transpired. For all I knew, they could've been the ones who left me. *They weren't.*

Anyway, as time went on, he continued to seem promising. He took me out a couple of days later, and we had a great time. I was then on spring break from work and he was in an off week from work, so we hung out several days in a row, and things were good. Too good. It was easy, something dating never really was for me. He met a couple of my friends. They worried he may not have enough of a personality to keep up with mine, but I was sure it was just because they met him so briefly, he just seemed shy and quiet with them.

The next week, he left to go offshore for two weeks of work. It seemed like maybe this would be good for me, since I tend to get sick of people really quickly. Maybe only seeing him every two weeks, for two weeks was a good solution to my problem. That first week, it really was. It was nice. He texted and called when he could, and I still thought I really liked this guy. So much so, that one night after drinking wine, on the phone with him, I invited him to a crawfish boil out at our farm the day after he got back in town. The problem here was that it was a family thing (Easter weekend), but I didn't really mean it to be like a meet-the-family thing. I just would be gone all weekend when he got back and thought he could just come with me. This probably wasn't really fair of me because I think he took it as moving things forward, which I really wasn't ready for. The second week of him being gone, I started to second guess everything. Spring break was over, I was done with drinking for a while, and he was really starting to get on my nerves. I thought back on it all and realized the times I had fun with him, I was always drinking and our sober texts really were boring and pointless. I decided to give it time because texting in general is boring and pointless, and maybe I would still like him. When he got back, I brought him to dinner with some friends, and he didn't say more than five words the whole time. We went back to my place and still he barely had anything to say. It was up to me to make conversation. I realized that beyond the first time he took me out, we really didn't have great conversation. We mostly were just drinking and watching movies (the wine and Gone Girl did get used a few days after we got them). So when things began, it seemed great because I love wine and movies. It wasn't until I took him out with friends or to the crawfish boil that I realized we really didn't have much to say to each other. Even on the drive to and from my family farm, we barely spoke. We relied on music to fill the silence, which again is confusing for me because I love music and constantly rely on it to fill silences when I'm alone. This shouldn't, however, be the case when you are getting to know someone.

After the crawfish boil, he wanted to clarify that we were exclusive, and I let him know that I wasn't seeing anyone else, but I also wasn't really ready for anything serious. (Mostly because I wasn't sure how I felt about him at this point and didn't want to lead him on too far this quickly). The next morning my friend came across his profile on Hinge (a popular dating app), and he was still actively using it, so who knows how exclusive he really wanted us to be. I think my favorite part was when I asked him about it a couple of days later. I really didn't care because I wasn't too clear with the exclusivity conversation so he had every right to still be on it, but when I brought it up casually, he chose to lie right to my face and say he wasn't using it (when the same friend had matched him and could see that he was still actively using it). Great choice, sir...

Humor is one thing I won't cave on. I need it. Laughing is my favorite. He didn't make me laugh. He wasn't very fun. He didn't even really think I was that funny. I'd make a clever joke, and I wasn't ever really sure if he didn't get it or didn't think it was funny. Either way, it was rude. When I wasn't drinking, it became painfully silent and agonizing to hang out with him. Easy quickly went out the window, and forced took its place. He left town again, and I was already over it. I had every intention of waiting until he got back to end things in person, but he must have sensed it was coming and decided the way he wanted to handle it was to annoy me and piss me off to make me do it sooner. He texted multiple times a day, multiple, unanswered texts in a row, many of which said the same things, but typed slightly differently. I let him know I'd become very busy and would respond very infrequently hoping he would get the point and fade away or at least back off a little. He didn't. He amplified contact. More texts. Follow up texts. Facebook messages because he thought the texts weren't going through. Can't make this shit up, y'all.

After almost a week of this, I couldn't take it anymore. I had to make it clear that it wasn't going to work (or it would've been two more weeks of this). He couldn't really make phone calls out there. He tried calling one night, and I thought this was my chance, but the call just kept breaking up (pun intended). So the next day he asked me what was up, and I just let it all out in a text message and said that I was just super busy and focused on me right now, and I wasn't really ready for anything serious (like I had told him all along, so it really shouldn't have been a surprise). He was offended and "knew something was off because he barely heard from me all week." *Uhhhh duh.* He said he was just disappointed that I didn't want to put in the effort to try to make it work because he really liked me, and I tried to let him know that if I wasn't willing to put in that effort, it wasn't worth stringing him along anymore.

I felt like I handled it okay and we could put it all behind us and move on. Unfortunately, we were Facebook friends, and turns out he had worse of a personality than I thought. He started to post every moment of his life, always. I have never seen a guy post like he did/does. I wanted to unfriend him, but felt like that was rude/it was kind of like a train wreck and I couldn't look away. It got worse over time, and he used more hashtags than I've ever seen one human use, and then liked his own posts. Liked his own posts. I repeat it because I want you to think that over. *Really, guy?*

Worst of all, a few weeks later, I let that same Hinge friend of mine talk me into trying out the app. One day after I created a profile, I got a text from you know who with the screen shot of my profile saying, in mature fashion, "Look who I found. I guess you're ready now :/" Come on man!! Have some dignity. I tried to let you down easy and you are taking every chance to remind yourself that I just wasn't that into you. Why must you insist on making it worse? As it turns out, him being boring was only half of the overall problem. Still, I'm sure you can tell from these stories of my life that boring just won't work for me. I need to laugh *with* my man, not *at* him.

A quick aside…

"Book Research"

Maybe the most fun thing about writing this book is that all along the way, I'm still out there. Fighting the good fight. Searching for someone who may just be the final chapter of the never-ending parade of tragedies that is my dating life. This actually creates quite a decent fall back plan for me to keep me distracted from said tragedies.

For example, when something new doesn't work out or I find myself regretting the previous night's decisions, I'm able to find a way to add it in to the book and chalk it up as research. This means that any time I find myself following some soon-to-be-memory back to his apartment after a less-than-frequent bar outing or feeling rejected after a much needed girls' night or being completely confused by a "Was it a date?" type of situation, I can always find some condolence in knowing that at least I can add it to the book. I am able to convince myself that there is a reason this crap continues to happen, and hope to everything holy that it is all going to work out in the end. It's all part of the journey, and what a journey it is.

However blissful this research can be at times, at others it is extremely frustrating. I find myself constantly wondering, "Why does it have to be so difficult?" I am *literally (*YES—I mean *LITERALLY,* not just being dramatic) out of single friends. I am out of ideas of ways to meet people. I've tried it all. No friends have anyone for me to meet. No one at work. I HATE meeting people at bars (if you don't agree with me on this after this book, we should talk). I have even tried some dating apps (obviously there is a chapter just for that, and we will get to that in more detail later). Life isn't a movie (at least not for me) where people just approach you at a coffee shop or the grocery store. People are freaking busy. They have plans and things to do. They're on their phone or on a mission to do whatever they are doing and get on their way. If they aren't, they probably aren't ideal for me anyway— as we should all know by now I can't deal with anyone who is too dependent. Point being: Where are people supposed to meet people?

Even more frustrating are unintentionally all of those coupled up friends who are full of advice. Don't get me wrong. I have truly amazing friends who have talked me through a lot of crap and dealt with me on whiney "I'm definitely going to die alone" nights. They are the best, and I almost always appreciate the complimentary lies they tell me to cheer me up. However, if we are being honest, there are certain clichés that make me want to rip my ears off. Happy couply friends, please take note:

There is no need to worry because there are so many great guys in this city*.* Or really any variation of "plenty of fish in the sea." Come on people, we know. This city is just so full of valuable options. Please, though, consider for just a moment that realistically the amount of guys who are in my age range, single, and straight and then narrow it down to the ones I'm attracted to, and it is actually a very small number. Now, take that number, subtract out the ones who aren't attracted to me. What are we left with? Say it's even 100 or so... Now let's think how will I meet any of them and will they be attracted enough/be single in that moment/have the balls to actually approach me? Again, not a movie. They are afraid of rejection or equally as mopey about only finding jaded/crazy/crappy girls or willing to believe girls will approach them or something. Whatever it is, they don't seem to take enough chances. Then they also want to complain about having to online date or just use it to hook up with girls. Here's a tip for guys: take chances and be more aggressive in finding what you are looking for in real life and eliminate the need for online dating. I know some girls are comfortable being the first to speak up, but there are plenty of us who still want to be pursued and feel like we are worthy of you taking that chance.

You won't die alone. You've got us. As thoughtful as their sentiment is, in all actuality it is in fact possible that I may not find someone. I know this is entirely well-intentioned, and partially true. However, the bigger truth to it is that you all will grow into your new lives with spouses and children, and I'll continue to feel left behind while I'm still single. So please allow me to sulk about this a bit, as it is a fair concern.

Relationships are overrated anyway. Great, thanks. That means a lot to hear while I'm at dinner with you and your boyfriend and one of you says it and the other laughs to agree and then you gaze lovingly into each other's eyes. It may be true, and there are certainly hard times within relationships, however this phrase is completely lost on me.

Please let me be the judge of whether or not relationships are overrated or worth it. I can't find even one, so I can't form a true opinion, but I'd like the option to decide it on my own.

Just stop thinking about it; you'll find someone when you least expect it. This may be the worst of all. It is so easy for you to say this when you are in a happy, committed relationship. Some of you were here at some point as well, and you, too, were extremely worried. Don't tell me not to think about it when you don't have to think about anything along these lines. At this point, every minute of every day is when I least expect it. If I were in a relationship, I wouldn't think about it either, but when everyone around me is and has no single friends for me to meet, it is impossible not to think about it and fear the impending doom of being forever single.

While we're on the topic, friends… Please don't talk about who you are going to set me up with if you aren't really going to or if you don't even know if they would be interested. Figure out if he's into it, and then make it happen. Or if you aren't sure, plan a casual meeting without anyone knowing that it is a setup. If they end up not interested and I know about it, it's one more disappointment I have to face and feel bad about myself. Just spare me. Please. It's exhausting and draining to get hopes up and be let down time and time again.

I know that my friends are extremely well-intentioned, but sometimes it is hard for me to get them to understand what I'm going through. Even when they went through bouts where they were single, they still at least knew what a real relationship was and were able to experience the positives of it. Unfortunately though, I can't afford actual therapy, so they are all I've got. Usually, they are great, but occasionally these phrases fall flat and leave me in a downward spiral. For this reason, I'm thankful for this writing therapy. My hope is that just one someone out there reads this and has felt these same frustrations. Not only so that I don't feel like such a complaining bitch, but that so someone else can find comfort in not feeling like the only complaining bitch out there when it comes to this kind of stuff.

Chapter 13

The Wedding Guy

"I stepped into a satin dancin' dress that had a split on the side clean up to my hip. It was red velvet trim and it fit me good."

Reba McEntire, *Fancy*

There comes a point along this lonely journey when you just need to break free and be someone else for a night. Someone who doesn't always make the right choice. Someone who just goes out with the sole intention of finding male attention, like a lame and basic bitch. I stumbled into feeling that very way one summer evening when attending a wedding.

A friend of mine from high school (okay, someone that I kind of had a thing with in high school, but then became just friends—*I know you're shocked*) invited me to go with him to a wedding. There had been a few times in the past where I was worried he wanted more than just friendship and still had feelings for me. So I initially declined his invitation to this wedding where I'd know no one else. He kept bugging me about it, though, as he had RSVPed a plus one, and the girl he planned on bringing was no longer an option. He assured me we would be attending just as friends and that it would be a really fun night. I repeatedly clarified to him that we were just going as friends, so that he wouldn't have any false hope or mixed signals regarding our evening. After agreeing to attend as JUST FRIENDS, I decided to make the most of it. I've never been to a wedding where I didn't know anyone, so really I could be anyone. The idea of it was enthralling. He had mentioned the couple had wealthy families and that the wedding would be "fancy as fuck." I searched out my most fun (and slightly slutty/slightly classy) dress, took excessive amounts of time getting ready, and made sure I looked my best. I downed a drink or two while getting ready and set out to see what the night would bring.

When I arrived to my friend's place, I met two couples who would be attending with us. Everyone was nice and fun, and we all had another drink or two before heading out. The wedding was downtown at a beautiful venue that doubled as the location of the ceremony and the reception. It was gorgeous and extravagant, and I decided to really just embrace the evening. I skipped the part where I normally feel awkward and insecure because I don't know anyone and the part where I think how terrible I am at dancing. I just grabbed a drink and hit the dance floor. I met people left and right and had a care-free blast. One groomsman in particular was really cute and kept making his way over to dance with me. We hit it off and continued dancing the night away. My date had plenty of friends there, so I knew he'd be fine. So I carried on with my flirting and enjoyed the reception, without a worry in the world.

I went on to drink way too much. Eventually the couple did their fairytale sparkler exit, but provided an after party upstairs at the same venue for their guests, as well as free

Whataburger snacks for the inebriated and famished. We partied on. I saw my date occasionally and danced with him a time or two, but ended up back with this new wedding guy. By the end of the night, the after-party felt like a hazy blue-lit club where everyone was shit-faced, maybe it was just me, but that's how I recall it. It finally ended, and the party would apparently continue at the hotel next door with all of the groomsmen who were staying there, so on we went. Poor choices, I know, but I wasn't me that night, so it was allowed...?

Eventually, I left the after-party with this guy and he drove us back to my place and came in to stay the night. While I'm sure the confident, free-spirited, no-consequences girl that I was that night instigated the idea of him coming over with less-than-pure intentions, once we arrived back and started to fool around, clarity hit, and it all felt too real. I had no idea who he even was and suddenly became viciously aware of that fact. I hadn't set my normal boundaries, and things were going too far with a stranger I knew nothing about. I'm certain that in that moment, I got very awkward and put an end to things quickly. I was suddenly tired and just wanted to sleep. Turns out, when it comes down to it, I'm not very good at being anyone other than myself.

The next morning was only slightly awkward, and he was nice about it. He lived somewhere far—Lubbock or Wichita Falls or some other random far away shitty town—so I knew I'd never see him again. It wasn't until he left that I realized I couldn't find my phone and really panicked that it was in his car or the hotel we partied in. Thank God it had made it home, and I just drunkenly managed to lose it in my room once I was there, so it turned up and everything was fine.

Eventually, I, of course, looked him up on Facebook. From what I could tell, he was definitely married. I'm hoping he was divorced, based on his actions that night. Maybe just separated? It was hard to tell, and I obviously didn't follow up any more on the matter. I felt sick about the whole thing (beyond just the hangover) and knew I wasn't that person, and couldn't be that person that lives without a worry in the world and pretends to be someone else. My worries are warranted and I'm skeptical for a reason—people aren't always great and keeping my guard up is part of who I am and how I feel good about myself and my choices.

Of course my date from the night was bitter and angry with me for a while because I left the wedding with someone else. He didn't seem to care that we attended the wedding as just friends, and obviously he was, in fact, hoping for more. In hindsight, it was not very nice of me to leave with someone else, and it's rather fair that he was mad at me. However, it was not my initial intention to become my high school prom date and just run off with someone else. It just happened, and somehow in my drunken mind I justified that it was okay because I had told him we were just friends. Like I've said before, I'm not proud of all of my choices.

I suppose there's nothing wrong with an occasional night like this to confirm that it isn't you, but I definitely felt sick about it for a long time after. It just made me feel stupid. A lot of these stories left me feeling guilty. Maybe I'm too hard on myself. Maybe other people aren't hard enough on themselves. Maybe everyone else feels as much guilt as I do, but doesn't talk about it. Either way, lesson learned. Be only who you are, and do only what you feel comfortable doing.

Chapter 14

The Party Boy

"He's the Devil in disguise, a snake with blue eyes, and he only comes out at night. Gives you feelings that you don't wanna fight, you better run for your life."
Carrie Underwood, *Cowboy Casanova*

Similar to Wedding Guy and myself the night I met Wedding Guy, Party Boy has no responsibilities. There are no consequences to his actions, and he does what he wants. This is someone to avoid at all costs. Sure, he's fun. Sure, he's probably attractive. What isn't attractive about a life without worry, where you just drink and laugh and have sex? Well, in fact a lot of things aren't attractive about it.

This isn't really about one guy in particular for me, it is more of a generic term for all of the idiots who drunkenly approach you in a bar. They are party *boys* because they don't act like men. They're wasted. They stumble over and spill a drink on you. They say something stupid to get your attention. They buy you a shot in hopes you'll sleep with them. They are out recovering from heartbreak, or they are just out being dumb with their friends. They are out alone because they refuse to grow up. They come over and dance on you without invitation. They take the drink out of your hand and drink it to be flirty… or because they are an alcoholic. They confuse a polite smile to be interest. They get your number and text you immediately to come over. They sleep with you and disappear. They perhaps have STDs or a girlfriend, neither of which should you want to fuck with. They are in a dark place and will take you down with them if you let them. Even when you're drunk, you can tell they are bad news, and you just want them to go away. They don't take no for an answer. They may be the one that sneaks a roofie in your drink.

They are beyond a project. You can't even pretend to see the good in them. There's nothing there worth fighting for; they're too far gone.

This is the guy you are allowed to hate the type. Hate the player, not the game. Tell to fuck off when "no" isn't working. Throw a drink in his face when he's being inappropriate. This is a guy who is not a good guy and is not in a good place. His behaviors and actions suck, and that fact should be clearly presented to him. He's on a personal journey of his own and needs to understand that this road isn't working for him or anyone that he's coming onto. Do us all a favor, skip laughing at love, and just laugh at him.

Chapter 15

The "Tinge" Chronicles

"Everybody's staring at their telephone. We've got the whole world in our hands and we've never been more alone."
Sean McConnell, *Rock and Roll*

If you've ever managed to find yourself in the world of online dating, specifically the swipe-to-decide-dating-apps, you probably have a few stories of your own. Well, I can honestly say that I've given it a try, really I have. But through it all, I came to realize that Tinder is just Facebook for penises and Hinge is just messaging for the mute. Despite my best efforts, I remain unimpressed by all of it, and by the concept as whole. I get the idea in terms of it being a framework for hope in your dating life. I can get on board with the idea that the apps put out there, like, "Hey, check it out. You aren't the only single human in your age range in the whole city, like it may seem." So, sure, it's appealing. However, let's take a few moments to delve into what you are actually getting.

I first gave Tinder a try about a year or so after it originally became all the rage. I'm a little behind the times like that. I trust no one and nothing, and it took a full year of not hearing of any Tinder murder streaks taking place in order for me to even agree to download the app just to test it out. I mostly joined it to see the appeal and to understand how it worked.

I went into it with no intention of actually meeting anyone. I was actually thoroughly embarrassed for joining in on these ridiculous shenanigans. More than anything, I was highly concerned that by having to log in with Facebook, that everyone in my life would know the moment I did it and make fun of me endlessly. In fact, I cautiously went through the steps to sign in slowly, pausing each step of the way to check Facebook and ensure I didn't need to delete some banner post letting the world know I had resorted to Tinder. Needless to say, Tinder and I were off to a rough start. I wish I could say we left on better terms than when I joined it, but I won't lie. We didn't even part as friends.

The first night, well week really, was extremely flattering. I started getting "matches" and guys were sending me messages. It was all very exciting. I was flipping through these pictures, taking my time to think "he seems like he could be a really nice guy" or "he looks like he's probably really funny." Ultimately, I was giving way too many humans the benefit of the doubt.

I quickly realized how easy it was to weed out the morons who chose stupid fucking pictures to represent themselves. Selfies of any kind (especially any in which you are standing in your own bathroom flexing your muscles) just aren't what I'm looking for in a man. If you are taking them just for this, then you're obviously putting way too much time and effort into a dating app and that bums me out. Why don't you have pictures of your real life with friends that you can crop yourself out of? And on the other side of that, hey dumbasses with ONLY group pictures—you aren't fooling anyone. Just be honest about who you are. Unless you don't know how to crop pictures… in which case you are too dumb to be in my life. What's with the guys only wearing sunglasses? What's wrong with your eyes? Do you have them? Are you hiding some elusive secret that your eyes in a photo will reveal? And what about the faraway guys? I actually love that you climbed a mountain, and I'd be super into talking to you about that except that every picture of you is so far away I can only assume you are in fact the Loch Ness Monster. Additionally, why would anyone think that it's a good idea on a dating app to only post pictures of you and your ex? This tells me you are either still hung up on her, your relationship was so long term and recent that she is literally in every picture in your life, or you are just too thoughtless and/or lazy to consider that it's not a great idea. All of which are indicators that I should go ahead and swipe left.

One summer, I decided to give dating apps a second try. Really more as book research than anything, but decided to go at it with an open mind and give it a real try. However, I opted out of Tinder this time around. This time, I chose to check out Hinge. It made more sense to me. It pulls from social media and finds people that know people you already know. The whole idea of meeting a "friend of a friend" seems like the proper way to meet someone, and this is just a modern spin on it, right?

I decided to also venture into OKCupid. This app didn't even last a full day on my phone because it was so terrible. I had heard some positive things about it, and I liked the idea that it asked you questions to narrow down the kind of person you are looking for, rather than just dropping you in a pool of photos and self-composed bios. It started off so promising asking simple, but important questions like "Are you a morning person?" NO. "Do you smoke?" HELL NO. "Which kind of date would you prefer?" etc...

After answering these questions (and panicking trying to fix the question where I accidentally clicked yes for smoking), I started to feel hopeful. I began thumbing through the matches and making my selections. Within 5 minutes, I had 50 interested people and, like, 20 messages from them. 5 MINUTES. How can you even begin to sort through 50 people, and if they just keep adding up... How do you keep up? It all just looked like spam and crazies because who would even notice that I joined in the past five minutes? Not anyone I'd be interested in dating. Get a life, people! I deleted that one within fifteen minutes.

That left me with just Hinge, and eventually I realized it wasn't any better than Tinder. I had so many matches that wouldn't say a word. Sure, maybe I'm supposed to say words first, and sometimes I would, but come on guys. If you matched with me, be willing to say something or don't match with me in the first place. I had struck up some decent conversations, but nothing really led anywhere. A couple of times I got invited on a date, but something didn't feel right.

I also tried Coffee Meets Bagel for about a week. It was too slow, and I was already overwhelmed by the other apps, so I was starting to lose steam and didn't put much effort into that one.

Eventually, I tried one more dating app: Bumble. It had become the most appealing to me at that point, not just because the guys on it were all attractive, but because it had clearly defined rules. The girl must talk first, which erases any confusion of who is supposed to message who. You have to just be confident in the fact that if he matched with you, he will respond to your message. On top of that, if you get match, you only have 24 hours to start up a conversation or the match disappears. This is nice because if you aren't willing to message them right away, you probably aren't that interested. Sure, maybe you were just busy that day... A guy then has the option to extend the match (a limited number of matches) for an additional day to give you time to say something (so flattering).

It was all very exciting again in the beginning, and I was feeling good about it. However, eventually I realized most of the guys are the same ones from all of the other apps. In fact, at one point, I got a match that looked promising, but couldn't shake the fact that he seemed really familiar. I looked back to Hinge, and sure enough he was one of the guys from Hinge I matched with, started chatting with, and then he just stopped saying words. I decided I wouldn't message him and let the match expire because he obviously wasn't that interested. The match expired, and low and behold, he messaged me back on Hinge: "Hey, I think we matched on Bumble too lol." Dumb ass. But whatever, I decided I would just roll with it, I didn't know how any of this shit worked, so fine, I'd play along. Witty banter ensued about why I didn't say anything in our Bumble match, etc... and we decided to go on a date.

A real life dating-app-date. I had to have a drink or two before I went, but I arrived to find a tall, dark, and handsome, witty, smart, and normal guy. We met up around 9:00 at one of my favorite nearby bars and ended up having about four beers each over several hours. The conversation was easy, the laughter was continuous, and he really was attractive. We decided around midnight that we were done drinking there, but he had a couple of friends at my favorite country bar down the street and asked if I wanted to go dancing. I casually agreed, but was really excited—what a fun date this had become. He was a great dancer, I hit it off with his friends, and during the last slow song of the night, we couldn't help ourselves from the cliché sweet make out, mid-dance. It was a great night. We ended up going back to his friend's house across the street, which was not far from my place. We drank, listened to 90's/early 2000's music, and played games. It was a blast, so I ended up agreeing to stay there with him that night. I laid the boundaries out to him that we wouldn't be having sex. He was cool with kissing and snuggles, and it was pretty damn great.

Everything was easy and comfortable, and that was a huge surprise to me. We got up the next morning, and since we were on my side of town, I drove him home (first we got breakfast tacos and coffee—the true way to my heart). He was going to the lake that day with friends so he got them some breakfast tacos, too. What a thoughtful guy. He wanted me to come in and hang out until they left for the lake, so I ended up meeting his brother and his best friend and we all got along great and laughed the morning away.

He had this way of making me feel desired. He couldn't stop talking about how he appreciated my athletic build and couldn't keep his hands off of me. Not in an obnoxious PDA kind of way, he just wanted to be near me. Even in front of his friends, he wanted to pull me close. It was really sexy.

They headed out to the lake for the day, and I went about my life with my friends. Heard from him briefly and he asked me to hang out the next day. When they got back from the lake, I went and hung out with him and all of his friends again. It was like he wanted to show me off. It was great. His friends were all wonderful to me and were so much fun. A couple of them made comments to me about how I was too good for this guy, or how it was so nice to meet me, they wished they would see me again, but that he would mess things up. I thought it was just friends giving him a hard time, but looking back now, I think they liked me as a person and were trying to warn me. Should have listened, I guess.

Driving back to his place, he made it a point to tell me how much he liked me. He warned me that we should take it slow because guys tend to lose interest after sex. (*This is a weird fucking thing for a guy to say, but whatever…*) I assured him I grew up with brothers and knew what guys wanted, and that I always take things slow anyway. He continued to tell me how much he liked me and how cool and beautiful I was.

Back at his place, we hung out with a couple more of his friends and he offered me wine from his giant wine collection (the other true way to my heart). I decided to not stay the night because it was a Sunday and he had work the next day, even though I didn't. I just figured it was easier to just head home that night. He walked me out, kissed me goodnight, and told me he'd call me the next day.

I never heard another word from him. Not one.

About a year later, I saw him out randomly and he was with some girl. He obviously didn't acknowledge me. I just bitched to my friends, who stared at him hatefully. Who the hell knows what really happened there? I never will.

With good reason, I lost a little faith in the dating apps after that. I agreed to one more date from Bumble. We went to dinner, had good conversation, and decided to hang out again. We made plans at dinner to go to a concert together a few days later. Again, I never heard from him again. I had been having phone issues the day before the concert, so I texted him the day of just to make sure the problem wasn't on my end, letting him know I'd had phone issues if he had tried to get a hold of me and I hadn't responded. He never said anything, which just made me look like an idiot for contacting him at all. Whatever.

Guys—Why bother to make future plans or tell me how much you like me if you're just going to disappear? Just say ok this was fun, bye. We can handle rejection. What we can't handle is being led on and ghosted by you fools. Then we don't know where it went wrong and it adds insult to injury when it comes to the rejection. Just don't do it.

That was the end of my online dating career. I felt more rejection than I needed to. It made me start to feel worse about myself, when it didn't need to. It seems like for the most part, people are on there just to find that comfort in knowing there are still options out there. Plenty of people have found someone and had it work out for them; I know a few who have even gotten married from it, but that doesn't mean you can force yourself to find someone there, no more than you can force yourself to meet someone in any other way. It's a fun way to pass the time, until it starts to make you feel negatively, then it's time to let it go and move on. *Swipe left, swipe right, delete and go out.*

Chapter 16

The Maybe British Guy?

"Mmmm, whatcha say, mmmm that you only meant well? Well, of course
you did."
Jason Derulo, *Whatcha Say*

This city is an amazing place to be. There truly are
awesome people and places here. You can meet so many
different kinds of people, eat *literally* any kind of food, and go
to a different coffee shop every single day of the year. It's
great. It should be, and often is, a single girl's dream. I have
had some exceptional nights out and met really fun people
all over this town. Sometimes this includes meeting people
of all different cultures.

Something I should note, I don't have the greatest
hearing in the first place. Therefore, when it comes to
someone with an accent, it becomes nearly impossible to
communicate properly. On more than one occasion I have
met some really great guys that I am tragically unable to
understand.

First, there was my trip to London. I worked for a
company for a very short period of time, but when I first
started they sent me to London for a conference. It was only
for a weekend, and we stayed in the hotel the whole time so

I didn't get to experience any of London. However, I did get to experience a tall drink of London water and all of the alcohol that they had to offer. I was still pretty young and drinking was encouraged. I had just left a company I hated more than anything for the first time, and everyone was extremely nice and welcoming. It was nearly too much pressure to drink and be fun with everyone else. I was just there to socialize with people from the other offices, and I'm great at being social. I was unfortunately a little too good at it, and hung in there with the best of them. I stayed up drinking well into the night with some bigger, older men who were pros at drinking. I showed them that American girls could hang in there. *Winner*. Not. I should have gone to bed a whole lot sooner. It was a new experience for me, though, and I just felt the need to take it all in.

Alongside me and the old guys was a 6' 5" beautiful creature. Easily one of the hottest guys I've ever seen. I was great at being social with everyone, but sometimes really struggled with what they were actually saying. If they had really strong accents, there was mostly just a lot of smiling and nodding, waiting for the moment when everyone else would burst out in laughter, so I could join in like I followed the whole conversation. Of course, this fine-ass specimen was one of the ones I could barely understand. We mostly just made eyes at each other across the table for a while, eventually pulling away from the group to play a game of pool, or as he called it "billiards." Just kidding, I have no idea what he called it—because I couldn't understand him. It didn't matter. We "talked" and laughed. By that, I mostly mean, he would say things, I would giggle and say "huh?" or "what?" only for him to repeat it for me to not understand again. Who needed communication when we could just gaze into each other's eyes? We ended up continuing to play pool for a long while until people started clearing out. As the crowd faded, our shameless flirting turned physical quickly. When we were nearly making out on the pool table, he "walked me back to my hotel room." By that, of course, I mean he came to my room so we could actually make out for a little while until he eventually stumbled back to his own room. It was extremely hot; *he* was extremely hot. He was exactly what you want in a random foreign encounter.

Needless to say, the next morning was not enjoyable. Many people missed or were late to the first morning meeting (including myself—employee of the month, and my mystery man). I showed up just late enough to miss out on coffee, which was obviously my punishment. My mystery man didn't show up until about halfway through that day. He looked like hell and he had a small red mark on his lip, of which I assume was a small bite mark. My bad, I guess. We made awkward eye contact, sheepishly grinned at each other, and went about our day. Ultimately after that weekend, we went on to never see or think of each other again (except to write this chapter, obviously).

It was clearly more than a physical attraction that had to be acted on. I honestly don't even remember his name at this point, nor does it matter. The point here is, the attraction was in the unknown and unexpected, not in the foreign accent. I could not understand the majority of the words he was saying. I don't know why accents are so hard for me. Most women find accents to be incredibly sexy. I just can't follow. Honestly, all I can ever do is laugh at them because my inability to comprehend is completely embarrassing.

The next encounter was a Midtown night out, I ended

up meeting some guy and staying at his place in midtown, I guess to make out a little and avoid paying for a ride home? It was another blur of a night out with my gay friends (and their boyfriends), and I maybe felt a little lonely towards the end of the night. I was obviously too drunk to realize that I couldn't understand him, but found him to be attractive enough to make out with a little. The next morning, I was confused about where I was and who this guy was. Turns out he was Colombian and still in school, not sure what for… something business related maybe? I couldn't understand much more, but I'm fairly certain he was some sort of drug dealer. He drove me home in his fancy car, while I pretended to be even more hungover than I really was so that I didn't have to try to understand what he was saying.

In his defense, he seemed like a decent guy and follow-up texted for while, attempting to hang out again. I was usually busy, and kept getting busier as his texts turned into weird anime memes. He also referred to me in every text as "Kilo-Jules," which he made a joke about being like the measure of energy, but it confirmed to me that he was definitely a drug dealer.

He texted me every once in a while when he was out to see if I was, and I never was. One night he walked up to me at a bar, and I almost didn't recognize him until he started speaking. He continued with sporadic texting for another month or so and then finally got the point and gave up.

More recently, my roommate decided she was going

to hook me up with her British friend. I knew from the start that it probably wasn't a great plan, what with my inability to comprehend English when spoken outside of an American accent, but she went on and on about it. I met him a few times, and he seemed fairly nice. I couldn't really hold a conversation with him without constant "huh"s or awkward laughter, so it wasn't a great start. One night we had all been out at a giant bar block party, and he Ubered back with me and my roommate and her boyfriend. I wasn't really drunk, and he was wasted. He ordered us tacos on the way home, and I thought, "Oh good, he has redeeming qualities then." He stayed at our place and was truly offended that I wouldn't have sex with him. He just kept saying dumb shit in his British accent like "But I want to put my dick in your mouth." (I hope you heard it in the accent, because it's one of the most atrocious things I've heard). *By this point, SIR, even if there was a chance of that happening, now it will never happen because who says that?* He definitely solidified my distaste for British accents and guys for good.

Another potentially less-exciting story involved my mother and I going out from drinks before a football game. Two guys had been making eyes and smiling for a bit. They eventually came up and started talking to us, brave and to the point, which I appreciate. Until the words came out. The one closer to my age was British (bye!) and the older guy was Scottish, maybe? They were super nice guys, but I can honestly say that I couldn't even follow along with the conversation because only about half of the words they said sounded like English. My mom fared better than I did, but we both agreed we had to get out of there. The British guy handed me his card and told me he'd love to hear from me. I tried to throw it away as we walked out, but my mom insisted that I give him a chance. I texted him the following evening. He responded 21 hours later (no, I am in fact not being dramatic) and said it was "nice to get my message" and in reference to the game we had gone to that he was "Sorry they lost! I heard they're pretty pants," but that "We need more daytime drinking sessions." I was out after that. Not only did he take entirely too long to answer me, but then I didn't even understand the words he typed out. It would've never worked out. I never replied back. Sorry mom, I tried.

I'm not hating on people with accents in general, just making it clear that I'm not destined to end up with one. It just takes too much energy to try and understand… Energy that I'm not willing to spend on guys I have mediocre to piss-poor experiences with.

Chapter 17

The Texting-Challenged

"I know you've been up waitin', waitin' for me to finally call. Talkin' dirty, it ain't what you really wanted. To slam another phone up against the wall."
Cross Canadian Ragweed, *Fightin' For*

There is apparently a world-wide epidemic that affects unsuspecting men and leaves them occasionally unable to respond to text messages. They are able to begin a conversation just fine, but then something happens when you reply to them, and they are suddenly rendered text-paralyzed. It must be so frustrating for them. I'm certain they have every intention of responding, because they started the conversation, but this ailment keeps them from being able to do so.

It seems unfair to blame them or grow frustrated, since obviously this is out of their control. However, we, the recipient of the original text, become affected as well when we feel the excitement that this person must be interested, come up with a witty response to give them the opportunity to continue the conversation, and then are left in silence.

As of late, I have encountered a couple of guys who suffer from this condition.

I met one out at a bar one night (my favorite place to meet people…not), but he knew people I knew, and he actually seemed to be really great. We hit it off right away, and he was completely charming. He got my number and asked if he could take me out. I agreed, and we hung out a little while longer. Things all seemed to be great. He texted me on the way home to see if we made it home okay. I waited to respond, because we were still amid a Jack-in-the-Box run when he texted. As we got home, he called. I answered reluctantly, and ended up in laughter when he said he was just calling to make sure I didn't give him a fake number. Long story short, he seemed super into me and I was pretty excited about meeting him and couldn't wait to hang out again. He texted the next day, but the conversation quickly faded out, due to his lack of response and seemingly low interest. Additionally, it was difficult to keep the banter up when he would say things like "Wayd." It took me almost an hour after he sent it to decide that it wasn't a typo and had to look it up to find that it means "What are you doing?" Between this and his short responses, I didn't put in much effort. I'm not one to keep bothering if you don't seem like you want to talk.

A couple of days later, I hadn't heard back and grew frustrated that his interest could have completely disappeared without reason, so I thought hell, maybe he's just clueless, and I'll attempt to fix it. I struck up conversation, it went well for a bit, and started to fade. I decided I didn't want to continue struggling to keep him interested in a texting exchange, so I just wrapped it up with "Let me know if you want to grab a drink one night this week." He had mentioned several times wanting to take me out, but when it came down to it, he hadn't been able to ask, so I stepped out of my comfort zone to do the work for him and face the possibility of rejection because for whatever reason I really liked this guy. He responded with "I have a softball game over by you on Wednesday." Vague and unhelpful, but I tried to make the most of it and said, "Cool. Wednesday works for me." I was proud of how I handled it for about 3 minutes until his response came across my screen: "Good to know."

Good to know. What in the actual fuck? If you don't want to hang out with me, 1. Don't ask for my number and tell me you want to take me out. 2. Don't text me first. 3. Don't give me a day when I ask you about it. I guess I should go easy on him since he clearly suffers from this texting disease.

Despite how enraged I was, I thought I would give him the benefit of the doubt, and thought maybe he will get it together. I was really on my game the night I met him, so maybe he was just trying to play it cool. Or maybe he was just a dumb oblivious boy, but that he would come through in the end.

Wednesday afternoon rolled around, and I hadn't heard from him. I started to think I wouldn't hear from him. I thought, "Oh well! At least I tried." Around 4:30 he texted: "Hey." That was it. Seriously. I had half a mind not to respond, but went along with it, to only receive more half-hearted texts letting me know his softball schedule, without giving me any kind of indication of how that affected me. I prompted with, "Okay, so we will meet up after?" and he let me know that was fine or I could come watch his games if I wanted. No thank you. I will not go sit by myself and watch a guy I don't even know play softball. I told him I wasn't going to do that, but to let me know when he was done and we could meet up.

Eventually, I got a text that they were heading to a bar down the street from me. At this point, I could no longer be a victim of his texting-challenged nature. I simply said, "Is that an invite?" Because really at this point it didn't seem like one. He "laughed" and said, "Sorry, yes it is." I met up with him and ten of his softball buddies for a drink. It was fun, and again he seemed interested. I got along with all of his friends. He was attentive and affectionate, but not over the top. It was actually quite ideal. We casually talked about weekend plans and tentatively set up a time we would be able to hang out.

He texted the next day, again showing interest. I kept it going as long as I could without being bothersome, and again it faded away without him making any kind of plans to see me again. Friday rolled around and again he texted first. We came to the conclusion that we would hang out Sunday. Here I am, the following Monday, typing this out and have yet to hear from him. I just don't understand. It's not like I'm whiney or care much that he blew me off; it's really just more about the fact that I'd rather he hadn't wasted my time and emotions for a week if he wasn't that into me. Don't act interested, don't text me, don't kiss me and tell me I'm a good kisser (I mean do because it's appreciated, but don't), don't make plans to hang out… if at the end of the day you are just going to disappear. It's a waste of his time as well, so it just doesn't make sense.

****

Similarly, I met a good-looking fireman out one night. Nobody was drunk, witty banter ensued (my favorite) and we had people in common that we both knew. He made it point to tell me how nice it was to meet a girl so pretty that was also smart and funny. It seemed promising, and he got my number. He actually followed through and took me out on a date.

As most of my first dates do, it went really well. It took up almost an entire Saturday and three different locations. Conversation was easy and alternated comfortably between funny and serious as we got to know each other. He thought it was really cool that I was writing a book, and I thought it was really cool that he was working on writing a screen play for a show. He told me about it, and it sounded pretty interesting and entertaining. We seemed to have quite a bit in common, and I felt like things were going well.

We parted ways close to dinner time, as we both had other plans afterward, but the date was really fun. There I was with yet another guy that kissed me and made it a point to tell me what a great kisser I was. I told him I liked that he was funny, and he told me he'd talk to me later and we would hang out again soon.

Disease struck and I never heard from him again. If I didn't know any better, I'd think someone was going around after my dates and threatening these guys' lives if they ever talked to me again. However, I do know better, and the guys are just idiots. One of our mutual friends ran into him a few weeks later and asked him what happened when we went out. He told him he really liked me, but that I had my life together too much. He didn't feel like he was good enough to take me out again. What does that even mean? Shouldn't you be with someone who wants you to be a better person?

What a waste of my time, sir. If you wanted a dumb bimbo, don't make it a point to act like you are so excited to meet a smart, together girl.

****

Again, I will say I hate texting as well and get bored of it quickly, but I just don't understand why bother going out of the way to text in the first place if you aren't going to continue with what you started. Texting someone gives the impression (rightfully so) that you are thinking about that person and wanted to talk to them. Therefore, if you don't want to talk to them (or hang out with them ever), then don't text them. It's rather simple in my eyes.

This must be a fairly new illness because I have really only seen such extreme cases recently, but it's been fairly frequent: three or so guys within a couple of weeks.

Yes, I've been meeting more guys recently, thank you for asking. I have gotten into really great shape thanks to CrossFit, and apparently my confidence radiates and guys have flocked. They've all been fleeting, though, as most have had this texting disease, others are too arrogant and/or dumb to hold meaningful conversation with. So the added attention is nice, except when it results in this extra confusion. Obviously, it's much easier to just not care, so I just let it go. However, I feel obligated to include it here, because it is silly and frustrating, and key sign that the guy is probably not great news.

In conclusion, someone should find out the cause of this

terrible ailment so that we are able to find the cure so that no one else will have to fall victim to this any longer.

Chapter 17.5

The Communicating-in-General-Challenged

"Why'd you call me today with nothing new to say? You pretend it's just
hello, but you know what it does to me to see your number on the phone.
Now tell me, what do you want... What do you want from me?"
Jerrod Neimann, *What Do You Want*

One of the other guys suffering from this wretched
texting imbalance is a guy I know through Crossfit. I met him
when I first started and had a serious crush on him pretty
quickly. He coached a run club on the side that I started
going to. He was quickly one of the nicest guys I'd ever met.
He was friendly, kind, supportive, funny, and encouraging. I
obviously wanted to like him, but we became Facebook
friends and I saw that he was unfortunately married. Of
course. No biggie, I could deal with that. Well, time went on
and later in the year he started to seem flirty, and I wondered
if maybe their marriage had been on the rocks or something.
Sure enough, a few months later, his FB status changed to
single. Crap. There was that crush again.

There I was again, attracted to someone I really
shouldn't. I played it cool and kept it friendly, but I couldn't
help but shake the feeling that he was flirty with me. I

convinced myself he was just a nice guy and I was reading too much into it, but really I didn't feel like he was that way with other people. Eventually, months later, we had a CrossFit beach day. We drank and played yard games and sat out in the water. It was a really great day. Somehow this guy and I ended up mostly just spending time with each other, and again he was flirty—I swear! We bet lunch on our horseshoe game, which I ended up winning, so he bought my lunch when we all went out after the beach. We then made plans to go see a movie when we got back. No one else wanted to join, so he bought tickets for just the two of us. We had about fifteen minutes when we got back to town to get ready for the movie. I ran by the store and grabbed some tiny wine bottles to sneak in because we couldn't get tickets to the theater he wanted to go to where we could've drank wine. I showered quickly, and he picked me up a few minutes later. We drank wine (after we had already been drinking all day) and enjoyed the movie. He then drove me home, but instead of calling it a night, he parked on a side street by my house. I asked if he wanted to come hang out and he suggested we go the restaurant right across the street. We walked over, split a bottle of wine and he ordered a few appetizers. Now, readers, be honest—this has all the makings of a date, right?

To this day, I still don't know if it was. I didn't hear from him after and at run club the next Wednesday it was just normal friend stuff, so I thought, "Okay, that's fine. I'm good with just being friends. No big deal."

However, he developed the aforementioned illness where he felt the need to text me randomly, sometimes several days in a row. At gym socials, it would usually end up with just me and him hanging out (and I wonder if anyone else wondered if anything was going on there). Sometimes the texting would last a while, sometimes it was one and done. Why text me when you are "coffee shop working about to head home" unless you are thinking about me and wanted to text me for no reason to ask "what concerts [you're] missing that night," assuming I'd be out at one? It was almost like he wanted to be interested, but just couldn't get there fully. Either way it was confusing and misleading when those texts would pop across my screen.

This confusion only got worse as time went on and we became better "friends." He occasionally asked if I wanted to go to dinner or a movie (usually after run club or CrossFit). Sometimes he would invite just me, which is very date like (especially when he offers to buy expensive wine for us to drink). Other times, he would invite me, but emphasize that I should "bring whoever" as if to solidify the fact that it wasn't a date and that I shouldn't come alone. One night, he invited me and "whoever" to come over to his house for dinner. I took my friend Anna and it was a delightful evening of friendly conversation, small amounts of wine, and delicious food. Fine, we're just friends. I get it.

Then more confusing texts, flirty banter, and hanging out outside of the gym. One night, he came to a Halloween party with all of my friends. I had organized a murder mystery dinner party at one of our friends' new townhouse, to distract everyone from wanting to go out so that I could avoid the misery that is Halloween. It was an absolute blast. The murder mystery was hysterical, the company was even better. I'm not sure anyone actually ate food, but the drinks were plentiful. All of my friends at this point knew the story and confusion behind "run club coach" and were obviously on my side, but quickly pointed out there was no denying his interest. I guess I decided I was over the whole misperception of the actual mystery that was our friendship, and just decided I didn't care. I had a blast with my friends, got way too drunk, and since he and I were basically acting like a couple the whole night (witness' words, not mine), I decided *what the hell, I'll put an end to all this will they, won't they shit for myself.* I just went ahead and put myself out there, basically threw myself at him. So we finally made out. He was nowhere near as drunk as I was, so yes, it was probably humiliating for myself, but I was tired of wondering *what if.* Although he went along with it momentarily, he made some comments about how things like this always mess up friendships, and we shouldn't take the route.

Cool. Just friends then. Feels good. Haven't heard that before. Just what I was hoping for: another single male friend who isn't interested in dating me. Bitchin'. Whatever, at least I got my answer, right?

Then why did he insist on texting me every single day after, almost in a forced "we're still friends" kind of way. Why it was so important that we stay friends, I'm really not sure. In what world does a 35-year-old single man insist on being friends with a 26-year-old single girl, when it doesn't involve sex? He's a nice guy, and I actually do think he means well, but damn. It was way too complicated and it really didn't need to be. See you at the gym, and that's it.

Luckily, he started dating another girl I'd met at run club, and I really liked her. It's much easier for us to be just gym friends, and even easier to be friends when there isn't the added pressure of both parties being single.

Chapter 18

The Coach Crush

"I am trying not to tell you, but I want to. I'm scared of what you'll say, and so I'm hiding what I'm feeling, but I'm tired of holding this inside my head."
Colbie Caillat, *Fallin' For You*

Speaking of CrossFit. Confession time. TRUE LIFE: I'm in love with my CrossFit Coach … or run club coach, or personal trainer, professor, etc... The struggle is all too real in this type of situation, and I know I'm not the only one who has been in this situation. It's really problematic because it's a hot-ass guy encouraging you, telling you how great/strong you are, and making you a better version of yourself. It is a very slippery slope for anyone. It's easier when they are not single because you can distance yourself from fantasizing about them. It is also easier if they are douchey and not a great person. I'm pretty sure it would also be easier if you have nothing in common. However, it is not easy when he's adorable, passionate, and has the nicest ass you've ever seen in your life—seriously, sometimes it's hard to focus on what he's saying.

I feel like this is a tricky situation in any similar circumstance, where a hot guy is in an authority position. Or maybe I just have an issue with being attracted to authority figures? Is that not normal? Maybe I should see someone about that. I'll add it to the list of topics for my future therapist. Either way, I feel like it's fairly common, especially with CrossFit. I've been a member of two different gyms, and at both gyms, I saw this phenomenon in action.

At the first gym, there were a total of three-fine ass male coaches. You find yourself enjoying their classes the most, and signing up for them as much as possible, after all—you end up working harder in their classes and getting the most out of it. Ultimately, there are plenty of situations in life where everyone is playing a certain role to make the wheels go 'round, and this is one of those situations. In this scenario, these coaches are playing the role of supportive, attractive, just-flirty-enough trainer who genuinely cares and sees the best in you. It's a very fine line they have to walk, especially because most of them really do care about your progress, really do see the best in you, and want to help bring it out. There's really no issue with this, if it ultimately helps you become better. The problem is, when this encouragement and interest comes out in the form of flirting; some do it in on purpose and some on accident. The other role is the client role. We play right into it as well, and it's helpful for us. They're hot and encouraging, you bet your ass I'm going to bust my butt and do as well as I can. If they believe in me, I'm going to prove them right. It works. It's why we like their classes the best. If everyone understands their roles, then there is no issue. My roommate and I would constantly chat about them and we knew there was nothing that would happen, but it's fun to crush on them, and it's helpful for your progress, so where's the harm? It was also helpful when they had girlfriends, because it is a quick easy reminder of the roles. Only one of them didn't have a girlfriend, and there were times I wanted to think that one day, just maybe... Then one day he called me the wrong name. It was a snap back to reality that you are just a client, and also that he wasn't all that great. Unicorn status dwindles... The other two really were great, and he was mostly a tool, but when you're in the gym-- and people are hot and single-- sometimes you lose sight of that. There is usually something to keep you in check with your role, and everything is usually fine and problem-free. The issue arises when you start to question those roles or, even worse, forget about the roles altogether.

The roles can start to blur as you're there for a while and become really involved with the gym. You are there all of the time, and slowly the role changes slightly and you start to become friends. This is precisely what happened for me. I genuinely cared about him as a human. So when he broke off to start his own gym, my roomie and I always saw his passion and knew we had to be a part of it. We whole-heartedly joined and became extremely active in the community from the beginning. The more time you spend with him, the more you just love him as a person. We felt for him when things didn't work out with him and his girlfriend, and we made an effort to get him back out there into the social world. This included not only social events that the whole gym would take part in, but also us taking him out to concerts and making him have fun. It was all on a very platonic level, and done with the intention of friendship. Unfortunately, though it also damaged the understanding of roles a little bit because we became friends in the process.

As anyone knows, single male/single female friendships aren't always the easiest thing to navigate. Luckily, I have had plenty of experience in this my ENTIRE life, so it was fine. It just sucked sometimes because as we would both complain about being single to each other and to the people around us, sometimes it seems like the easiest solution would just be to go ahead and date.

Obviously, it wasn't an option. It would be a terrible idea, but damn it's hard to shake sometimes. Especially when his job is to tell you how great you are (it's not his job when he tells your roommate how amazing and beautiful you are and she tells you about it—which really made things confusing). People would ask me why we didn't just date each other and I know people had to have said similar things to him, but at the end of the day he wouldn't date a client. Perfectly fine. It makes the most sense. Why risk damaging the love I have for my gym and all of the progress I've made because of him when it probably wouldn't work out anyway, but damn—that ass.

So, instead of risking the inevitable failed relationship, compromising our entire friendship, we just went on comparing dating stories and complaining about how hard it is to meet people. Luckily, he eventually found someone and again, that always makes things easier. It's then that you can clearly see then the reasons why it wouldn't have worked out anyway, and we were always meant to be only friends. Sometimes you just want the shortcut though, when it seems like such an easy option.

Ultimately, in hindsight it would never really work. I knew that, but right there in that moment, when the feelings hit, you just can't shake them. When that happens, what you really need is...

Chapter 19

The Distraction

"Baby, be my cigarette buzz. Let me drink you 'til I get drunk. It's been a painful day, be my Novocain. Nothing gets me high like you, makes me smile the way you do. Help me turn off my brain, be my Novocain."
Sean McConnell, *Novocain*

When you're on the lonely train, sometimes you end up hopping aboard a crush train that you can't seem to get off of. You find yourself hung up on someone inappropriate or someone you can't have. You want someone or something so badly that you cling to any small possibility that something could be there (see the two previous chapters) and you just want to believe it could happen. Then you torture yourself day in and day out over-evaluating everything they do and say, in case there is a thread of hope (see the two previous chapters).

It's at this point where the only way out is to find a distraction. Literally, ANY man who can take away your attention from the situation, and give you someone else to think about. He doesn't have to be the one, just someone that grabs enough of your attention so that you are able to snap out of the stupid crush that's consumed you. This can be found in a number of ways.

You may find yourself visiting a flirty waiter at a restaurant you frequent. Maybe you see a guy at your favorite coffee shop every once in a while. Perhaps you use the dreaded dating apps. Or maybe you get all dolled up and head out for the night, if not successful in finding a distraction, at least you'll end up with a sassy picture of you looking all sexy to prove you don't care about that dumb crush anyway.

However you find this distraction, you know it's not going anywhere, but it's fun and necessary. Maybe you go out with them, maybe you don't. That's not the point. The point is literally to get it in your brain that there are in fact other humans besides that crush; they are out there. They may or may not be interested. You may or may not be interested. But the possibility is there. The attraction is out there. Allow yourself the opportunity to find it again, and stop destroying yourself about something that just isn't going to happen. If someone isn't pursuing you, why obsess over wanting to be with them anyway? The CrossFit coach himself once said, "Who wants to tell their grandchildren one day, 'Well I wasn't really sure for a while if Grandma was the one but I thought about it for a few months and then I decided sure why not?'"

If it's not there, it's not there. It's so easy to say, and so hard to accept. Especially when loneliness sets in, but it's true. Everyone deserves to feel wanted, and everyone should when it comes to finding the person they'll decide to spend their life with.

One of my distractions was a guy I'd known since high

school. He was flirty back then, but nothing ever really happened. We went to different schools and never really saw each other. He resurfaced every once in a while, usually after I posted a good picture on Facebook, and acted interested again. He was one of those CrossFit douches, who was totally self-involved, but he also was in the marines for a while and had a 5 year old son, so I thought maybe he had grown up a little. He resurfaced at one point, when I desperately needed a distraction. I decided to give him a chance this once. He came over, we drank some wine and just chatted for a while. He is an extremely attractive human, I can't deny that. So attractive, that as he talked, I tried so hard to pretend he wasn't an idiot, asshole, and douchebag. I just kept downing wine, hoping that he would get more interesting and that the dickish things he said about his family and pompous things he said describing himself and his coaching skills would disappear. I hoped him talking shit about my CrossFit coach and belittling our gym was all a joke and that he would take it back and apologize and just be normal and kind. I drank enough wine to decide to make out with him despite all of this, but not enough to invite him to stay over. It was a damn good make out. His body and his confidence made for a really fantastic ten minute kissing session, and for those ten minutes everything he had said and done that night didn't matter. No one else mattered. Life was good, I felt desired, and my crush disappeared for ten minutes. After those ten minutes, he left and I was able to see clearly that no matter how great someone appears, no one is as perfect as you make them out to be. That crush that you have may be a jackass in disguise, or just not right for you. Either way, it was enough to pull me out of the crippling crush at the time. Things obviously didn't progress for us. He still texts and checks in every once in a while when I post a picture on Facebook that he likes. I typically don't respond because there's nothing there, but it's a nice distraction and moment of flattery when I may need it from time to time.

There's nothing wrong with a little distraction, as long as you aren't leading someone on who's developing real feelings. Lucky for me this one wasn't. Most likely, he just needs a little distraction of his own every once in a while. Or this is how he treats all girls, as disposable and sparing encounters. Who's to say?

Chapter 20

The Musician

"He has a poet's soul, and the heart of man's man. I know he'll say that
he's in love, but between you and me, he won't be good enough."

Tim McGraw, *My Little Girl*

By this point, everyone in the world should know better
than to date a musician, but also we should all still be able to
agree that plenty of them are tragically attractive—even the
ones who aren't attractive. In college, I wouldn't say I was a
full on groupie, but my love of music sometimes got
confused with a love for musicians.

I attended concerts weekly. I honestly still would if it
weren't exhausting and expensive. My passion for the way
music can move people and heal people is immense. It's
amazing how people can find the words to tell their story in a
way that can touch so many others. It's incredible that simple
strums of a guitar or fingers on piano keys can make people
feel those words deep down in their bones, their blood
pumping in time with the melody. There's such a raw
honesty to really well-written, truly inspiring music, and that
overwhelms me.

Therefore, it's no surprise that I find it completely
attractive when people are able to write music that moves
me. In college, this led to me being front row at hundreds of

concerts. Now these were mostly fairly small to medium size Texas Country music concerts, held at bars or small outdoor venues. Some shows smaller and some bigger, but none were more or less important to those guys up on the stage, or for that matter to me.

There's something comforting in noticing the roles we play in life, and truly becoming an active participant knowing the importance your role plays. Musicians are playing the role of captivator. They are literally trying to reel you in and get you to buy what they have to say. The purposeful eye contact and well-timed winks are a critical part of their show, and it's a beautiful thing to take a step back and admire how good they are at what they do. It's pretty cool how they put everything they have into each show to play a certain role for their audience.

Meanwhile, young, fun girls play just as critical a role: admirers. Concerts would be nothing without them. Smiling, dancing, and singing along are all essential. If these girls didn't make their way up to the front and really get involved, the artist wouldn't be able to put on the show they've prepared. I, of course, was one of these admirers. I played my part. I sang along, pointing as the best lyrics came out, to let them know they really nailed it, hell I probably would've even winked back if I could have. You get caught up in these moments. Even if it's a smaller show, and only a couple of hundred people know their name, you can't help but feel fan-flustered when they put on a really good show, and find a way to make you feel like you were a part of that energy,

We always ultimately made our way back to the merchandise tables late in the night, waiting until the lines had mostly died down so that we could take pictures, get autographs, and of course when they were single, to get in some one on one chat time, you know, just in case. I met, befriended, danced with, and kissed some really fun singers, drummers, bassists, lead guitarists, harmonica-and-keyboard-players, merch guys, and sound guys. I took shots (and one nap) on many a tour bus, got drinks bought for me by musicians, and ended up with more picks, koozies, and signed drumsticks/t-shirts/towels/posters than I could have ever imagined. It was the time of my life.

Of course, as I grew up, I realized musicians are bad news for those very reasons. It's too tempting when the role you are playing is to gain young, drunk, female admirers. They aren't always bad guys (though some are), but it's too fine of a line to walk, especially when you're meeting them while in your designated roles. Meeting them out of that role or (even better) before they are really out there touring is the best way to go.

I'd like to say I fully outgrew the musician fascination, but not long ago (at age 26), I went to a show with my old concert-running-buddy, and ended up leaving the show with a date the next night with the bassist of a new up-and-coming band. I guess I can't help myself. Turned out the precious guy was only 23 and just about to really start touring all over the place, so it was destined to go nowhere, but it was really nice to drink a few beers and chat music with him for a couple of hours.

In the end, I know I'm not meant to end up with a musician, but I'd like to think whoever I find will have the same love and appreciation for music. Or perhaps precious song lyrics are the reason my hopes are too high for men in the first place, and music will always be my only true love. Who knows?

Chapter 21

The Speed Dater

"And I've been livin' with the loneliness, it's got down in my bones I
guess. It's just another phase of being free."
Turnpike Troubadours, *Good Lord Lorrie*

There came a point while writing this that I felt like I had
to be sure I was trying it all before I could fully whine about
the lack of finding what I'm looking for. I needed to be all in,
and after taking the online dating app approach for a while, I
knew I was almost there. A friend of mine decided it would
be fun to try speed dating. I'm pretty sure at some point in
my life that was something I swore I'd never do. If I had a
dollar for every time I swore I wouldn't do something and
then did it anyway...

I reluctantly agreed, mostly because she really wanted to
do it, and I thought, "What the hell. What could it hurt?" We
got ready together and had some wine before we went. We
arrived way too early (on time) and went straight for the bar.
I befriended the bartender while we waited, so he knew this

was the first time I'd done this and needed the drinks to keep coming. He'd seen this event before and wished me luck and promised me wine. Not to spoil this chapter, but he was my favorite person I met that night.

They rounded us up and explained the process. As I looked around, I was incredibly confused by the options we were about to meet. As it turned out, my friend had chosen a "Christian" speed dating event for ages 25-39. I was 26 and my friend was 28. All of the guys were well over thirty and all but maybe three of them were Asian. I quickly downed my drink to get a refill before heading back to the table to get things started.

We each received a piece of paper to track our encounters. Each person was assigned a number, and as that number came around and met you, you wrote down their name, and anything you wanted to remember about them. You had five minutes, they would ring the bell, and the guys would rotate to the next table and you'd have a new conversation for the next five minutes. The only problem was that it wasn't a new conversation. It was the same one over and over and over. These guys were taking it so seriously, it made uncomfortable. Dates often feel like job interviews, but this was like a job interview on crack.

Picture this: *A 35 year old Asian man, sitting inches away from you. Instead of a drink in his hand, he has a pen in one hand and the paper in the other as he begins to write in the boxes (you've yet to write down a thing) and through his glasses, his serious gaze sets in on you and asks, "What does Christianity mean to you?"*

I don't mean it to sound like I'm making fun. This is probably a very logical way for some people to meet.

However, it was not what I had in mind. I was completely dumbfounded and unprepared. I held back my laughter and tried to honestly discuss my feelings on religion being a personal thing, and how organized religion and churches don't play as much of a role in my faith anymore. He vigorously wrote down my answers, as I attempted to make eye contact with my bartender buddy to plead for a fresh drink. Five minutes have never felt so long, and a couple of times, I almost got up and rang the bell myself because it was truly painful. I smiled and tried to be polite/ maintain sobriety and composure, because although none of this was my cup of tea, it was obviously important to these people.

I counted down the number of blanks on the page until we were back to the beginning and when we finally made it, they announced to us we needed to circle on each number if we would like to contact them again: YES NO or MAYBE. I looked down at the blank page, but a big circle all the way down all 15 rows in the NO column, tipped my bartender well, grabbed my friend and ran. I took her to a bar and met up with some friends and made a decent night of it.

The next morning I received an email from the Speed Dating people, letting me know the names and emails of the people who said they wanted to contact me. They said "Although you circled no, maybe knowing their interest, you'd like to reach out." Then below they had pasted in from a spreadsheet all of the names and emails of 14 men. Number 8 had not circled YES. I don't recall which one he was, but I found myself slightly offended for some reason.

I deleted the email and have had to unsubscribe multiple times from them trying to get me to sign up for another speed dating event. Sorry, speed dating, you are not my thing.

Chapter 22

The Big Game... I've Still Got It

"'Cross my arm is that old ink stain, God I wish I could erase that name...
Now I question every road I've taken, and I regret every heart I've
forsaken. Here's my confession. The mistakes I've made are coming
back to haunt me, like a ghost from the grave, always there to taunt me."

Eli Young Band, *Skeletons*

I hope that by now I've made it clear that despite
wondering if I'll ever find someone to love me, I truly enjoy
my independent lifestyle. I only know how to plan my life
around me, and I am completely uncertain of how I'll ever be
able to work someone else's life into mine. I love being able
to take up my whole bed at night, laying in an L-shape so I
can fall asleep to Friends re-runs on my TV. I constantly
need to have car concerts, where I'm allowed to sing horribly
at the top of my lungs. I enjoy being able to talk to my dog
like she understands me (because she does). There's
nothing I love more than taking thirty-minute baths whilst
jamming some tragic music, drinking wine, and honing my

acting skills by pretending I'm in some heartbroken nineties music video. Most importantly, I have a very strict TV schedule to adhere to/ long list of Netflix to marathon, most of which are shows I'm embarrassed to admit I watch, let alone try to get someone to watch with me. There are so many parts to my life that are everything I want and only work because I'm single.

That being said, I'm sure by now I've also convinced you that part of me craves finding that person who will allow me to stay me, while also helping me find the road to compromise and selflessness that I know I need in my life. For someone like that, I believe I could make a few small changes. Surely, I could manage to share a king size bed with someone. I could reserve my car concerts for when I'm driving alone to and from work. I'm certain whoever my guy is loves dogs as much as I do, and will understand the need for said conversations. Love ballad bath time will have to remain my time, I just can't compromise there. However, half of my Netflix list (okay maybe a third) are guy type shows that I could easily curl up with someone to watch and would enjoy then spending hours discussing/debating opinions about them. Point being, now that I know myself well enough to know how to make myself happy, I sometimes think about how ready I am to have someone by my side to enjoy life with and continue to grow as a person.

The problem arises when I decide amidst my carefree single life that I'm ready for a little positive attention, and there's just none coming my way (because as we've read this entire book, I don't have the easiest time finding male companions). I can deal with the fact that my one and only isn't in my life yet, but sometimes I just need the occasional reminder that "I've still got it." –A game that my now sister-in-law invented the summer her and my brother were broken up. It wasn't so much a game, as it was get ready, go out, and make sure people still hit on you. All women need this from time to time, no matter how confident, sassy, or independent (really even those in relationships could use it occasionally). No, it isn't about feeling validated based on your looks. It's just a nice reminder that your spark is still there, and allowing yourself to feel good about that.

When the need for one of these nights arises, we call it a girls' night and hit the town. We've learned to keep girls' nights small. It seems to prove less intimidating for guys to approach, and it's much easier to manage where to go and what to do. It usually ends up being just two or three girls and we bop around taking turns buying rounds. For the most part, these nights end up being wildly successful in the "I've still got it" game. We usually end up, at the least, with a free drink or two and some decent conversation. Of course, we also end up with some great stories, lots of laughs and some extra unwanted attention.

However, just recently, I went out with a few friends from college to watch one of our Alma Mater's more important football games. I wasn't necessarily in an "I've still got it" needy kind of place, and was just excited to watch the game. The original intention was a "girls' night" kind of day with my key wing-woman Tamara, who's fiancé was out of town. Whenever he leaves town, she's determined to find me a man (and probably enjoys a few "I've still got it" moments of her own, as she should). She's cute, fun, approachable, and loyal/ forthcoming about already being taken—all of the qualities you can ask for in a wing-woman (see examples in other various chapters). However, as plans progressed, we had a few other friends show up, including some guys, so our original plan was foiled. Nonetheless, we really were focused on the game and excited for the day of drinking and fun.

Our Aggies were playing Alabama, our most hated rival, and we really needed to win. We all saddled up to the bar at an Aggie watch party and went all in on buckets of beer and carafes of mimosas (yes, both—don't judge). Despite having guys with us, we still managed to earn some free drinks from a guy at "the coach's table." We're still a little unclear on what that meant or what they were there to do, but we graciously accepted. Since the game was going horribly, our bartender decided our free round would be "sadness shots." The game at this point was a disaster, so we all agreed. Unfortunately for me, shots these days never fare well. They usually just make me too sleepy and/or sick and want to go home, but with just the right amount (one), I become a college level party-timer again, ready to rage all night. When this happens, I almost always end up saying or doing something stupid that I feel negatively about for a few weeks, not to mention the three days I spend feeling like death because I can't recover from the deathly hangover. Thanks, bartender. Thanks, mid-twenties. Thanks, 2:30 kick-off time.

From there, things escalated quickly, and by things I mean level of drunkenness. We wandered down the street to another bar for more buckets and shuffleboard. Tamara's fiancé was getting back in town that night, so we stayed out for him to meet up with us. By the time he arrived, I believe we were the definition of shit show. One of the guys with us is a close friend of Tamara's that I just met recently. He's fun, cute, and nice, and every time we drink we are super flirty with each other, but nothing really ever happens there.

By this point in the night, the two of us were all but making out. In fact there were apparently bets among the others that it would happen. Tamara bet against it though, knowing by now that it's just harmless flirting that's going nowhere.

After a few more rounds and games of shuffle boards (with some strangers this time), we started to come to the conclusion that we'd call it a night and head home. I was about to take an Uber home with everyone back to Tamara's, but just as we were about to head out, I struck up a conversation with a very tall, handsome man near the bar. Now, just to clarify, at this point, I was teetering the line of blackout like old times (and earlier chapters) and I'm unclear on how this encounter took place—it's possible I just walked up with the confidence that comes with an all-day drunk fest and forced him to talk to me. Either way my friend Anna agreed to stay with me so I could pursue this hot dish.

Fuzzy turned to darkness around that time…

I woke up in darkness, confused with a throbbing head, and wondering where I was and who was next to me. *Classy, I know.* All I knew was that I had to pee incredibly bad and had no clue which darkened doorway would lead me to a bathroom. I was too afraid to wake this human to ask because I couldn't seem to replay the night in my head far enough to be sure of whom I went home with. Lucky for me, we know by now I am not a fan of random sex, so it wasn't a concern of feeling dirty in this moment like I could have, but it was more a concern of who is the human… AKA what do you look like and is your personality horrid?

My friend Jen and I also had another game in college. It

was based off of a popular game show called "Press Your Luck," where contestants gamble with their fate and yell out, "No whammies!!" to avoid losing everything. She and I had always been embarrassingly addicted to game shows, so we watched it frequently and equated it to our social life and us pressing our luck on drunken nights. We would wake up the morning after partying to recap our nights, and as we pieced the night together, we would joke "no whammies, no whammies," in hopes that we didn't do anything stupid or hook up with someone terrible. When we could confirm that there was a hot-ass guy involved, game show style cheering would take place.

So there I was, 26 years old in a dark room, saying to myself "no whammy, no whammy, no wha—aw, to hell with it!" I sat up quickly, and as I hopped up out of the bed to avoid the situation at hand, asked where the bathroom was. His voice trailed off as he gave directions that guided me into an excessively extravagant bathroom. I'm talking giant standing glass shower that rained down from the ceiling, huge garden tub that I could have some serious jam sessions in, a closet the size of my kitchen, the works... As I wandered far enough through the fanciest bathroom I've ever seen to finally make it to the toilet, I thought, "Crap, did I go home with another Colombian drug dealer?"

I peed for what had to be nine minutes, and the whole time I was looking out of a giant third-story window and could see the Downtown skyline from an angle that seemed entirely unfamiliar to me. *Great, where the hell am I?*

I decided on my long (15 second) trek back to the bed that dignity was already lost, and I just had to face what I'd done. He was awake now, and I just needed to focus on what was important... like did I make it here with my phone, wallet, and Tamara's second earring (only one was currently in my ear).

I confidently marched through the door as I came up with a good opening line, "So where am I?" as if the information really meant nothing to me. *Nailed it.* I shook my head at my idiotic choice of words as I lay back down in the dark beside him. He rolled over, laughed, and said, "Not far from Midtown. Oh and I'm Will..." with a precious grin on his face. I heard Jen and the game show audience applauding as I had not hit a whammy, but rather the jackpot as I remembered meeting this tall drink of water at the end of the night. I gave myself an imaginary high five, impressed that this hunk wanted to take me home. *I've still got it...*

We blew past the awkwardness and just decided to embrace the cuddling and get to know you conversation happening synonymously. He began to "jokingly" express frustration about my unwillingness to remove my pants the night before. I smiled unapologetically and mumbled something about what responsible choices I make. However, in these situations, I'm just not sorry. Guys take a girl home because they want sex. I go home with someone occasionally because I want a warm body to wrap me up in their arms and make out a little. Why is the guy's reason the right way? Why am I a tease if I'm getting what I want out of it? Get over it. I'm sure plenty of other girls who are into random sex have given you exactly what you want. This was my turn to get what I wanted.

He continued to give me the opportunity to remove my shorts, *so thoughtful of him,* I know. We decided to settle for some cuddling and witty banter, which was my ideal situation for a hungover Sunday morning. We began to replay the night, and I made it clear that the sadness shots were to blame for my overt drunkenness, and how this was all Alabama's fault for beating us. He agreed and blamed "'Bama." He nodded along as I ranted about their terrible fans and stupid Nick Saban. He echoed my sentiments with, "Yeah, Nick Saban is the worst… (*paused for a moment and then*) …You do remember that I'm a 'Bama fan, right?" Horror music cut through the silence and played loudly in my ears, as I tried to comprehend this ridiculous moment that fate (and whiskey) had muddled up for me. My eyes darted to the night stand to see the dreaded Crimson A on the coaster near the lamp. *Fuck*. I am *literally* sleeping with the enemy on the eve of a tragic loss.

Again, we powered through the awkwardness, and talked a little longer (his idea was that he wouldn't take me home until I finally took my shorts off). Overall, he didn't seem that bad: responsible, stable job, solid group of friends… Nothing demonic like I imagined of 'Bama fans. I finally located my phone and the second earring, but no wallet. Fate decided to give me a break on that one though, as I checked my phone to find a missed call and two texts from Anna- one reading "Where did you go?" and the other "I have your wallet." I immediately text her back, thanking her and apologizing for disappearing, still unclear on how it all transpired, but having been informed by this guy that we did in fact just disappear.

I also had a text from some random number, a guy I guess I had played shuffleboard with that said, "Hey it's the Longhorn." (This was ironic in a strange way because the Longhorns were the Aggies' previous rivals). *For shame.* Our texting banter didn't last long though, as his text messages started using words like "sucka." Additionally, I had another missed call from my friend Matt (also a

Longhorn, but that isn't relevant), who was supposed to meet up with us at some point, but between the two of us being drunk-asses, we never were able to find each other. His missed call was accompanied by a voicemail. I listened to it, curious about what it said (and because I'm slightly OCD and don't like having unopened red notifications on my phone). His voice echoed loudly through the phone speaker as he shouted into the voicemail, repeatedly yelling my name at 1:30 AM: "GOD DAMMIT! NOW... NOW THIS IS A BOOTY CALL BECAUSE YOU DIDN'T FUCKING PICK UP EARLIER! DAMMIT... Dammit (*Quieter*)." It is by far one of the funniest voicemails I have ever heard. I was laughing pretty hard and when it ended, I just looked at 'Bama guy, shrugged and said, "That was just my friend, Matt." I don't think he enjoyed it as much as I did. Maybe you have to know Matt.

Later that day, I picked up Anna and my purse and took us to lunch and to pick up her car from Midtown. I was telling her about the voicemail and had to play it for her about four times on speaker in the car because we couldn't stop laughing. She also got a ridiculous voicemail that night from a number in Senoia, GA. All it said was, "You got the money? I got the druuuuugs." We couldn't breathe for most of lunch laughing at the ridiculousness of the night. I got another good laugh later that night when Matt called me back a little drunk, when he remembered leaving the voicemail, just to make sure I had heard it. I had to share with him the fact that I shacked up and that the guy had gotten to hear it, and of course, told him about Anna's voicemail. Neither voicemail will be forgotten.

In the end, sleeping with the enemy wasn't quite as soul-crushing as I'd imagined. He was gentlemanly enough to drive me home (after holding me hostage for most of the morning), but I guess he didn't care much for Aggies either, as he forgot to get my phone number. Who cares, I've still got it. *(Insert sassy red dress emoji here.)*

Chapter 23

The Setup

"A thousand miles seems pretty far, but they've got planes and trains and cars."
Plain White T's, *Hey There Delilah*

There are apparently so many people pulling for me to find a man. Truly, it would shock you how many. Despite how this book makes me sound, I'm not an entirely terrible person. I literally have people tell me that they are praying for me, keeping their fingers crossed, and are out there searching on my behalf, determined to help me find THE ONE.

My biggest fans are often my friends' parents. It's like they see into the future and can tell I'm wife material, but guys don't see it or aren't ready for it. Or maybe that's just what they're saying to make me feel better about it. This was often the case growing up, too. All of my guy friends' parents would tell me how they hoped I would end up with their sons.

Through this process, I end up getting plenty of offers

for setups. Sometimes they are followed through on, sometimes they aren't.

In one particular case, I had a woman I work with constantly on the lookout for me. She sought one out for me at one point and was ready to set me up. She came to me telling me all about this guy she met who sold her jet skis at their new lake house. "He's sooo sweet, and sooo cute. Just absolutely precious. Such a good guy." She just knew we would hit it off.

She got me to agree to meet him and gave him my number. He texted me one day and started up a conversation. It didn't take long and of course we both wanted to know what the other looked like. We each sent a picture of ourselves (which is strange in itself). It all felt so forced and uncomfortable. He told me how beautiful I was and the picture he then sent was cutting off half of his sunglass covered face to fit his dog in, but his dog was cute. I could tell he was short, but whatever. Pam said he was a good guy, so I'd give him a chance. We texted back and forth and eventually tried to make plans to hang out. It was then I realized that she bought these jet skis almost an hour north of where I live. No. That's way too far. That's a freaking long distance relationship. I don't even like to leave the loop, let alone drive an hour to go on a date. I immediately knew that was the end. He made a few attempts to hang out, and I felt bad because Pam tried to help me out, but it just wasn't going to work. Nice guy or not, it's just not something I'm willing to compromise on. Add it to the list of unforgiveable flaws. It's one thing if you are in a relationship, and someone has to move; trying to make a long distance thing work is worth trying at that point. However, I am unwilling to start out long distance, especially for a blind date.

I love people's good intentions and appreciate the genuine concern in wanting to help me. Setups are such high pressure situations, though, especially if a friend is involved and you feel bad letting them down. I just got really awkward and ignored it until the problem went away. I'm sure somewhere he's writing a book about what confusing bitches girls can be. Oops! I just didn't want to waste his time or lead him on when I knew it wasn't going to go anywhere. At least I didn't first go on and on and tell him how much I liked him and couldn't wait to hang out, and then ghost on him.

Chapter 24

The Real Deal

"And all that girl wants to be is loved. Yeah, all that girl wants to be is
loved."
Josh Abbott Band, *She Will Be Free*

When you've gone through as many crappy dating
situations as this, you start to lose hope that what you're
looking for actually exists at all. You start to wonder if maybe
your mom is right and you are too picky. That asking for
respect, thoughtfulness, and humor is just too many things
for one guy to possess at once.

Then, as if from nowhere, when you least expect it, just
like everyone promised, it surprises you.

One night, I was having one of my need-to-look-hot-and-
find-a-distraction nights. I was drinking at brunch all day, and
meeting up with friends to go out that night. Though a little
buzzed already, I managed to take a quick nap and pull
myself together and look quite hot. Along with Jess, Anna,
and Brandon, I went out to a random dive bar, ready for a
fun start to a raging night. The bar was pretty dead, and not
the crowd we'd hoped for. We called Matt to see what he
was up to. He had just returned to his place with a crew of
friends who had just left a concert, and invited us over to

hang out with them. So we grabbed an Uber and headed over.

At this point, I thought I knew all of Matt's friends. However, within the first few minutes of arriving, I was sitting on Matt's counter, chatting with him and Anna, when I noticed a cute guy across the room. "Who is that?" I asked immediately. "Where have you been hiding him?"

A few minutes later he came over, and Matt introduced us. We immediately hit it off and began chatting for most of the rest of the night. Brandon was sure he was gay, so I kept my guard up and later when we went out, I called him on it. He wasn't and ultimately we flirted, danced, and kissed at the bar we all went to. I ended up going home with him that night. He was adorable, and the way he looked at me was different than any other guy I'd known. I was smitten, and decided I should play it cool and head out before I overstayed my welcome. I called an Uber, and went to head out as the driver said he was arriving. As I got downstairs and out of the gate of the complex, the driver called to tell me he couldn't find me. Meanwhile, my phone was moments away from dying and I had no idea where I was. I quickly texted my pin location to the driver and to Jess, just hoping one of them would find me, and then my phone died. I stood outside in the middle of the street, in last night's dress and boots, hoping to God I wasn't going to have to go back in and ask this guy if I could charge my phone. Not that I could get back in the gate anyway. As I stood there debating asking a random neighbor if I could charge my phone, the Uber driver miraculously arrived and saved me from complete humiliation. I got to charge my phone, fortunately, but the price I had to pay was being asked a million questions by my driver about where I was, who I stayed with, when we met, and how things went. As the panic of the morning subsided, I realized that I really like this guy, but that he didn't get my number. I thought, "Well, maybe he'll get it from Matt."

Sure enough, two days later he texted me and asked me out. Normally dates stress me out and I have to drink to even attend them, but for some reason, I was really excited to go out with this guy again, no drinks needed. Over the next few weeks, he kept asking me out and we kept having a great time. Conversation was easy, dates were comfortable, and I never had to worry about when I would hear from him because I just knew that I would, and I always did. He opened doors for me, brought an extra jacket to outdoor dates in case I'd get cold, and tried to be creative with new date ideas. As time went on, things kept progressing and I realized just how much I liked him. Even sex, which is usually off the table because of insecurities and my lack of trust, he made comfortable and easy and ultimately amazing. He was thoughtful and caring, and unlike anyone else I'd dated.

I couldn't believe that I found a man this attractive, sweet, respectful, and funny. And he liked me! I was amazed that I could truly be myself around him, and he still wanted to spend time with me. Everything was easy and just kind of fell into place. I couldn't believe I'd actually found what I had been looking for all this time.

A few months in, I officially became his girlfriend. 27 years old, and no one had ever called me their girlfriend. I was on cloud nine. He met my family, our groups of friends became intertwined, and we started making plans into the months ahead. One night we were out and some guy told me I had a nice ass, and he got defensive of me and talked shit to him to let him know I was with him. It was nice to have someone be protective of me and proud to be with me. Things were going shockingly well, and I was loving it.

He made me laugh. He made my heart happy. He made me feel lovable and secure in my ability to have a relationship. I liked his friends. I wanted to meet his family. I loved how even though he was quiet and sometimes shy, he found ways to open up and reveal parts of himself to me to let me in. Any flaws or red flags that may have existed didn't matter to me. He was barely my height, if not almost shorter than me, and I didn't care. That's how I knew it was the real deal. I found myself bored at work sometimes doodling his name like a freaking school girl. I even caught myself for the first time in my life considering what kind of a wedding I would even consider for myself in the future, something I've never really thought about. I had it bad. Bad to the point where I was falling in love. I would say it in my head sometimes, but felt like it was too soon to say out loud.

We were coming up on six months and I couldn't believe it had lasted that long. It was around that time that I would start to get a little frustrated in the back of my mind. I felt like I was always having to make the effort to make plans. He wasn't ever big on texting, which I'm not either, but it started seemed like communication wasn't always great unless we were together. It almost felt like he was pulling away, but I didn't know if it was just us getting comfortable and complacent, and that I was reading too much into, which of course I always do. But then, one weekend, we were together all weekend, and for some reason he just suddenly felt so distant to me. I don't even think he kissed me that weekend. I started to get nervous and feel insecure about what we had, which was new and uncomfortable for us, and

I didn't like it. I tried to convince myself everything was fine because I was in love with him, and I wasn't ready for it to end.

Monday and Tuesday of the following week went by and I hardly heard a word from him. I asked him Tuesday after work if everything was ok. He said "Yeah, just have a lot on my mind and I got some bad news about my friend's girlfriend who found out she has cancer," and asked when I got done with my workout. The fact that he had a lot on his mind AND this other news told me that this news wasn't what he meant was already on his mind. Plus, he knew when I worked out. I started to have a slight panic attack on my way to the gym. I could feel it all crumbling away from me and I didn't know why. I texted Jess the screenshot and told her I was freaking out because if he broke up with me, I wasn't prepared for it. She tried to talk me down, and I calmed down enough to get through my workout.

Once I made it home, he texted that he was on his way, and everything about the way he was texting me felt like something was wrong. When he got to my house, he didn't come upstairs to my room. I knew then it was for sure happening. I walked downstairs and he stood across the room and asked how my day was. He never asked how my day was. I told him he was being weird, and he moved to the table, sat down and said, "Well I've been thinking." I knew it was coming, so I could be strong right? I sat down and let him go on to say, "It's been six months now, and I don't feel like my feelings are progressing like they should. When I try to think into the future, I just don't see it and I don't know why, but I don't want to string you along if I don't see a future." At this point, he had already started crying. I was trying to hold it together, so I just kept saying, "Ok." I got up from the table, went upstairs to get any of his things that were in my room and put them on the table, as he proceeded to apologize over and over. I managed to ask if there was somewhere it went wrong, and he had no answer. There had to be reason. I wish he'd just give me the reason. He kept saying he'd tried to come up with a reason and couldn't because they all just felt like a made up excuse. God, I would've preferred an excuse. Some reason. Something to blame or be mad at him for. Tell me there's someone else. Tell me I got fat. Tell me you hate my dog. Anything. But he gave me nothing. Just a good guy being honest about not wanting to be with me. I couldn't help but feel like I just wasn't enough.

I, of course, couldn't make it through without crying, so I held my face in my hands to hide to my un-makeuped ugly crying face. I told him that it just sucked for me because my feelings were progressing and I did see a future, but that I would try to see it as a positive, because at least now I knew that what I was looking for was, in fact, out there. He cried harder as I said that. It got to the point where the only sounds in the room were us crying, so I finally said, "Well, you're not just going to sit here and watch me cry so…." And stood up for him to follow me to the door.

At the bottom of the stairs, I opened the door, waiting for him to leave. With tears in his eyes, he looked at me and hesitated, edged the door shut and pulled me in for the final embrace. As he did, I smelled his familiar scent that I'd grown so attached to. His head fell to rest against my cheek. I could feel his eyelashes flutter against my face as he blinked away each tear. Our tears embracing each other and falling onto his shirt. He moved his forehead to mine and apologized again and again. Each time, I told him I knew he was sorry, and finally worked up the courage to say that he didn't need to be sorry because at least I was able to let someone in and see that I am capable of these feelings after all, and that I guess everyone has to have their heartbroken at some point. He again cried harder, and kept shaking his head. "I don't want you to think I don't care about you, because I do. I really do. I really don't want to hurt you and I know that's what I'm doing." This time it was me that cried harder. I pulled away and told him that wasn't helping things, and re-opened the door. Then, reluctantly, finally, he walked out the door.

Chapter 25

Over and Over Again

"I gave my heart, and you gave yours too. Nobody cheated and nobody lied, that's why I'm confused. There's no explanation, and there's no reason why, but it's closing time."

Sean McConnell, *Closing Time*

I would have loved to have ended this story with happy ever after. I would love to say that through years of miserable dating, I held out for greatness, found it, and didn't have to deal with the mess of dating any more. Unfortunately, I warned you from the beginning that I didn't have all the answers. If anything, after this I may only have more questions.

I was utterly devastated. It was brutal and unexpected. All I could think about was having to start this whole freaking thing all over again. I can't start over. I can't go on these awful dates. I can't wait ten years to find another decent guy. I've never felt that way about someone that felt that way about me, and then he just changed his mind. I was crazy about him and he seemed crazy about me for a while, and without explanation it was gone. He took it all away. How will I find it again? Do I even want to find it again, if it's just going to disappear like that without notice? It's exhausting.

I was left to sit around and wonder: What the hell went wrong and how does someone just change their mind like that? And if you really cared about me and it was so hard to let me go, then why do it? Did your feelings really stop progressing or did you just stop trying?

I had always pitied women for being so distraught after a break up. If he doesn't want you, then he's not worth crying over. It wasn't until this breakup that I felt the real pain of it all and understood. It was especially difficult because I didn't get a real reason. Nothing went wrong, he just decided that there was a time frame on love and he was out. All I needed was a reason to hate him and to be mad and I could've raged and gotten past it. But instead, he left me lost, confused, and blindsided.

As everyone promised, time goes on, and things slowly get a little easier, and it hurts a little bit less, but it really was devastating. I found myself thinking how much worse it must be when you get a divorce. Someone promises to love you forever and you think you're in the clear and then you have to start all over and you're left feeling broken.

Sure, I'm thankful that he was honest and didn't drag it out or make it worse, but I can't help but think that if he didn't see a future, then he probably didn't from the start, and why be with someone at all if you don't see a future? I dropped boring guy a couple of weeks in, as soon as I realized he was boring. Have the decency to end it before my feelings get that real.

As each day passed, and I started to find my strong, independent self again and ditch the weak bitch behavior that took over that first day, I was able to see things with some clarity. I could talk myself into the fact that I shouldn't have felt like I was the only one making the effort. I shouldn't have to wonder why he met my family and never really mentioned me meeting his. I never pressured him or wanted to rush things, but I should have felt a little more secure if it was the real thing. His friend shouldn't have had to bring up the boyfriend/girlfriend talk for us. He never really explained to me what happened with his past relationships. I often wondered because I didn't want something like this to happen, and sure enough it did. I should have also not always had to wonder why he liked me. I want to be with someone that tells me what they like about me and why they like to be with me. I don't need attention and compliments every moment of the day, but it's not that hard tell me I'm pretty or smart or funny every once in a while. I think he called me beautiful once on our second date, and that's the only time I remember hearing it. Maybe told me I looked nice one other time, but in six months, that's nothing.

Of the millions of people in this city, I, of course, saw him out that next weekend. Walking out of the last bar and toward an Uber with my friend, I saw his roommate, and went to say hi—immediately noticed him there too and turned and walked away. It was so bizarre to walk away from each other like strangers, like we didn't even know each other. It killed me. Of course he didn't see us the whole night, surrounded by guys, free drinks, and exchanging phone numbers. Oh yeah, that's what it's become again. The beginning of this book has started all over. Fun fact: the guy who got my number was same name number 5. Obviously it's not going anywhere (not just because of same name and because he lives outside the loop), but mostly because it was me needing a distraction, more than anything—because I can hardly bear the thought of being back to single, having to go out, looking for someone that's respectful, thoughtful, and funny. It's exhausting to think about, but I've learned something from each of these chapters and I continue to grow as a person. This time around, I'll know more of the red flags and warning signs and I won't have quite as many ridiculous stories. *I seriously hope not.*

Beyond the lessons I've learned for dating, I've learned a lot more about life in general.

Chapter 26

Moral of the Story

"After all of the darkness and sadness, soons comes happiness. If I
surround myself with positive things, I'll gain prosperity."
Destiny's Child, Survivor

When it comes down to it, what I realized from my first
real heartbreak, is that I'm surrounded by unbelievably
awesome people. In the last few years as I've grown more
confident and more clear on the direction I want my life to
go, I have managed to surround myself with amazing people
along the way. I am blessed with an incredibly supportive
family. My friends love me and want the best for me, and
even the ones that have moved on from the single life and
don't always understand or want to deal with my crazy
stories, were there for me in a heartbeat when they knew I
was truly hurting.

In the wake of being dumped, I had the biggest support
system that completely engulfed me. My sister-in-law let me
cry on the phone for an hour. Matt showed up immediately at
my door with ice cream and wine. My mom sent flowers and
wouldn't go more than a few hours without checking on me
and telling me how great I was, and how it would stop

hurting so much soon. Jess and Jessi took me out for drinks the next night to get me out of the house. CrossFit friends, future and past roommates, and all current friends checked on me, hugged me, went out with me to keep me distracted, offered to do anything I needed, prayed for me, and most importantly made me laugh again.

Laughter is the best medicine… It may be a seriously lame saying, but there is nothing that can help heal you quite like laughing with family and friends. It allows you to feel the joy in life again and to know and be reassured that everything is going to be just fine. Music is usually what heals me, but when I was hurting that badly, even music was breaking me with every emotion tied to every lyric and I couldn't turn to music. At least not my typical music. I had to ease in a jam/laugh as I sang along and danced in my car to Destiny's Child "Survivor" to slowly find my way out of that emotional drain.

My sweet first graders that I was teaching at the time were so full of love and hugs for me without even knowing what was upsetting me. It was amazing and such a comfort to my soul. My teenage volleyball girls didn't even know it happened, but it was the end of the season and the love and appreciation they had for me just for being their coach was completely overwhelming and made me feel so much pride and love for what I do. My dog curled up and snuggled next to me whenever a rough patch would hit me and I needed to cry some more. My brothers' concern for me was extremely sweet and made me cry, not out of sadness, but out of love for them and their genuine care for me.

I realized in those days that followed just how many other factors there are to each and every person's life. So often, we get caught up in defining our lives in the ability to find "the one" and spend the rest of our lives with them. The thing about it though is, "the one" could apply to so many other facets that make your life what it is. *The one* group of friends that mean the world to you and build you up when you need it. *The one* hobby –for me exercising- that brings you complete joy and allows you feel competitive and strong again. *The one* job that allows you to be happy and also make a difference, and feel a sense of purpose again. *The one* family that is by your side all your life and helps make you become who you are, while supporting you whether you're where you want to be or struggling to get there. *The one* pet that loves you and is there no matter what, making you feel unadulterated love. Or maybe it's the one house or car you've worked hard to buy. Maybe it's the one book you wrote because writing gives you a sense of wholeness and clarity. Maybe it's the one child that you created and gave life to and would give your life for every moment of every day. Maybe it's the one degree you worked hard for, paid for, and fought for. Maybe it's the one transformative life experience of weight loss, or career change, or vacation you've always dreamt of. There are so many elements of life that define who you are. If you allow finding a relationship to be the sole deciding factor of happiness, you're bound to end up in an existential hole (whether you end up finding it or not) and wondering how to make it through this thing called life and why even bother. There's too much more to life and every piece has to be taken into account to determine what life means to you and what you're looking for out of it.

There was something dark welling deep inside of me, and if I didn't have the other pieces in my life, it could have consumed me. It almost had me questioning the purpose of life, and the idea of starting over to find love felt truly sickening. But piece by piece those other elements in my life gave me a glimpse back into happiness and the love and support that surrounded me, put me back together and pulled me away from the darkness.

Like I said from the beginning, I don't have all the answers. Dating is not easy, but all I can say is that if you create the life you want and surround yourself with goodness, you'll at least be able to *laugh at love, when life laughs at you.*

"For as much as she stumbles, she's running. For as much as she runs she's still here. Always hoping to find something quicker than Heaven to make the damage of her days disappear, just like Guinevere."

Eli Young Band, *Guinevere*

www.ingramcontent.com/pod-product-compliance
Lightning Source LLC
LaVergne TN
LVHW022322080426
835508LV00041B/2025